OF CATS AND KINGS

BY THE SAME AUTHOR

I & CLAUDIUS

OF CATS AND KINGS

CLARE DE VRIES

BLOOMSBURY

The people I met in Burma risked their lives telling me about
themselves and their country. To protect them I have changed
their names and the towns they came from.

First published 2002
This paperback edition published 2003

Bloomsbury Publishing Plc, 38 Soho Square,
London W1D 3HB

A CIP catalogue record for this book
is available from the British Library

ISBN 0 7475 6384 5

10 9 8 7 6 5 4 3 2 1

Typeset by Palimpsest Book Production Limited,
Polmont, Stirlingshire
Printed in Great Britain by Clays Ltd, St Ives plc

ACKNOWLEDGEMENTS

Many thanks to the people who helped me before, during and after the journey:

Susannah Bates, Tanya Bunnag, Liz Calder, Martin Clutterbuck, Lisa Crosley, Dana Dickey, Judy Feller, Allan Offerman, Madeleine Rampling, Vivienne Schuster, Sophy Shand, Kymberley Sproule and the Regent Resort and Spa, Mary Tomlinson, Sally Kemp-Welch, Piers Whitley, Jim Woods.

Thanks also to the many NGO organisations in Chiang Mai who need to remain nameless in order to continue doing their good work for the Burmese refugees. Thanks also to the people I met in Burma who were brave, helpful and kind in spite of the difficulties they face daily.

For Peter Kemp-Welch

CONTENTS

PART ONE

ENGLAND

CHAPTER 1

LONDON

I AM SITTING in 192 in Notting Hill waiting for Matt to arrive and nursing an over-priced glass of red plonk. I am nervous. What if he doesn't show? I peek at the door each time it opens. I have a brief chat with a girl I know. She insists on telling me the history of her hair from the age of fourteen onwards. Then Matt walks in. His black eyes and brown-black hair glint broodily as he takes off his coat. Our eyes are on each other as he walks towards me.

I wish this was our first date and not our last. That the last few months hadn't been full of emotional disappointments and bad sex.

'Sorry I'm late.'

'OK, darling.'

Kiss kiss, hug hug.

I tell him how it is. That it's been a year since the death of my beloved brown Burmese cat, Claudius, whom I lived with for twenty years, and I think it's time to move on and get another cat. That after months of dithering I am finally going to Myanmar (Burma) to search for aforesaid Burmese cat and Siam (Thailand) to search for a Siamese. That my unquenchable wanderlust has finally got the better of me.

I don't tell him that we are through, regardless of whether I leave or not, and that mooning around London waiting for Love after we're through is not my style. That I can't bear that every friend is getting married, shackling themselves to a deluded and compromising security, as far as I can see. That I don't wish to find myself in yet another unsuitable relationship with a man out of boredom or peer pressure, and that it is far wiser to get a cat to love instead. No, I'm not getting married. That's not my style. Not that I've got the choice.

Matt's reaction makes it clear that I have jumped ship literally seconds before being chucked overboard anyway. He agrees, in fact cares far too little for my liking.

As he goes for more cigarettes I look round at the other men coming in. As yet unable to shed my years of boy-seek training, I swap glances with them, barely-disguised seconds of 'Is that you? Are you for me?'. It's the hope I can't bear. Let me take you through the last three disasters before Matt, which were like watching a train wreck.

The first saw me in the grip of a hideous addiction to beauty treatments, colonic irrigation to be precise. I wasn't really happy unless someone was sticking a hose up my bottom and draining me of several months' worth of chips and mayonnaise. My first treatment was the day of my fifth date with Orlando. I wasn't stupid enough to admit that I'd just been cleared out of £80 as well as a few other things as I sat opposite him in Zilli, Soho that fateful night, but the menu did force me to admit there was food I now couldn't eat; like dairy and wheat.

'I've got candida, you see.'

I smiled proudly.

Later (three hours, to be precise), when he was absolutely refusing to do the business, I had to find out why.

'Your sexual disease,' he replied.

He clearly thought I'd said chlamydia.

The second saw me opposite Casper in Fish! Having asked for the lobster, only to watch the chef chop it in half, alive, in front of me, and then wang it on the grill, while its legs shook and waved like a demented spider as they sizzled on the fire, I then had to listen to Casper, caught in some bizarre upper-class mating ritual, reel off his family tree back to William the Conqueror. He waited patiently for me to do the same. I was brought up in Streatham.

Later, when he walked me home, I invited him up for a drink.

'Maybe just a snifter,' he replied.

After stilted conversations and an adverse reaction from Claudius, my beloved Burmese cat, who as my catometer was definitely telling me that Casper was *not* The One, Casper decided to leave.

As I showed him the front door, through a communal hall that hadn't been painted since the war, and whose thirty-year-old carpet, frankly, stank, he suddenly pounced on me Octopus-style leaving nothing untried: he pinged my bra, tousled my hair, and wedged my knickers between my cheeks like a bike. He then scuttled off and I never heard from him again. Thank God.

Many months later, disaster three saw me dumping my new Spanish boyfriend at La Famiglia in Chelsea. Our short but passionate time together had been marred by the fact that every time we made love he called me Linda. When I later discovered that this was in fact Spanish for 'pretty' I didn't regret my move, because the frothing at the corners of his mouth during this our last date alerted me to the fact that he had taken an E. So did his standing up and shouting, 'I love all of you,' in dusky tones to the entire restaurant.

Back at the bar, cigarettes in hand, Matt decides to slip into old-friends mode immediately, and hack my idea to death.

'So, let's get this straight, *you* are thinking of travelling to Burma?'

'Yes. *Me.* Do you have a problem with that?'

'Ha! Hahhhhhaaahahahaha!'

He doubles up howling, and slams his hand on the bar, simultaneously crushing his cigarettes to death, I am happy to say.

'Why not hit Persia and Constantinople while you're about it?' he continues, looking round first at the glams.

(*Friends*-style layered hair, bubble-gum-pink sequinned hem skirts, cowboy boots or stilettos, too much cleavage showing through translucent black tops, and sparkly eye shadow), then at the bohos (paisley scarves tied Russian peasant-style around heads, flairs flamencoing around legs, second-hand coats orange as Belisha beacons, plastic Mexican shopping-basket handbags). Normal trying to be whacko. Or glamorous. Or both. The men look smug – they know they're in demand.

Matt turns back and downs his dry martini, wincing slightly.

'Actually, Burma and Siam, or Myanmar and Thailand, as those of us *not* stuck in some strange twenties time warp in the mistaken notion that the old names are more glamorous call them, couldn't be more different. I suppose you know that Burma has been in the grip of a military junta since 1962 and is very isolated?'

Of course I know. But I smile evenly in an attempt to stem the oncoming flow of scorn.

'Ah, you didn't know, I can tell from that silly benign sainted look you always put on when you haven't a clue. Well, it is. And have you heard of Aung San Suu Kyi?'

'Oh Matt, for God's sake, you're not in court now, stop cross-questioning me.'

'Have you heard of her?'

'Of course I have.'

'She is a Nobel Peace Prize winner. She advocates a policy of tourism-boycotting because the money from most tourists goes straight into the pockets of the military generals.'

'I've thought of that. I just won't stay in government-owned hotels. I'll travel in private cars and stay with families. That way I'll ensure the people get the money.'

That shuts him up for a bit. But not for long. He orders a vodka.

'You'll have to slum it. You're a comfort kitten. You won't be able to go around chugging back margaritas, you know.'

'Of course not. They won't know how to mix them properly.'

'You go to pieces when you get caught in the rain. What about squats for loos? No hot water? Mud and slime from the rainy season?'

'Really, Matt, I'm made of tougher stuff than that.'

'Except whenever the going gets tough you go shopping. You won't be able to do that in Burma.'

'Don't be ridiculous. There are hundreds of markets. In fact I'm going to Mogok, which is famous for its jewels, to buy a sapphire to match my cat's eyes by. Royals have sought jewels from Mogok for centuries, I suppose you already know. Anyway, it'll be easier once I'm in Thailand. I am going to search for my talisman in style. I shall be carried in a sedan chair by servants, I shall have picnics on white tablecloths, eating from silver cutlery. I'll be borne aloft by elephants.'

'Elephants? OK.'

'Elephants. Exactly. First class the whole way. Sherpas.'

'*Sherpas*?'

'What?'

'They don't have them there . . .'

'Oh. Well, anyway, I shall eat garlic and lemon daily to make my blood unpalatable to the mosquitoes. How do you think Isabella Bird managed, or any of the nineteenth-century female explorers? In short, by the time I reach Bangkok, everyone I meet will be overbowled by my *loveliness*.'

'Ha!' he says morosely into his pint. 'If you're so smitten with other eras, centuries even, you'll have to travel without using mobiles and e-mail.'

'Why should I?'

'You're right, why should you? Be inconsistent by all means . . . But that merely proves my point – that you're mad.'

'Look. Why do all men refer to women they don't understand as mad? It's so annoying. Because I prefer to live with an animal rather than a man you all have to attack. You've missed the point entirely.'

'Yes, well, let's not row. You're clearly distraught –'

'Oh my God, could you *be* any more annoying?'

'So if you're going, I'd like to give you this to remind you of me and keep you company before you find your new friend.'

He fishes in his pocket, brings out a Biro, two battered glacier mints, copious amounts of fluff, and finally hands me a black sock with two white buttons sown on the end. The buttons have black pen marks in the centre.

'What is this, Matt?'

'He's my special friend. His name's Smoky. Look, he talks to you when you're feeling lonely. Hello, Smoky, how are you?'

Whereupon he inserts his hand into the sock, creates

a mouth with his fingers just under the eyes and starts to have a long conversation with Smoky, until everyone around starts staring. And he thinks *I'm* mad. Midway through his conversation with Smoky, he stops, his eyes alight, and turns triumphantly to me.

'I know why it's a bad idea! Because both Burma and Thailand have jungle. *Ha!*' He is delighted with himself. 'Have you forgotten *Belize*?'

Let us leave Matt spluttering in 192 and wander gently back in time to Millennium Christmas when we went on holiday together to Belize, our main aim being to stay with Matt's friend, Jimmy, who lived in the jungle.

We started off easily enough in Caye Caulker, in simple cabin rooms on the beach. We browned ourselves and then went to stay with the High Commissioner Tim David over Christmas.

I mentioned the Burma idea over breakfast on our last morning there and he was horrified by it. Horrified by the inappropriateness of looking for a pedigree cat in a country where the people were oppressed by a military dictatorship and often unable to feed themselves. However, he was not as horrified as I, when, during a moment's silence after this conversation, I let out a roaring fart, the likes of which I haven't emitted since I was twelve in school assembly. But from years of diplomatic training, he and his wife Rosie carried on eating their scrambled eggs and fresh melon, as though nothing had happened. I was mortified and looked to Matt for support. He gave me a distant glance, that delivered the firm message: Don't look here for friendship, sunshine. I don't know you. After attempting to stifle my giggles, I excused myself to run out to the hall corridor where my hoots of laughter shook the walls.

Immediately after Christmas, we went to the jungle. Matt felt it a good idea to ease me in gently to the lifestyle, so we started at a jungle lodge called Pook's Hill. The whitewashed thatched cabanas had running (hot!) water. After a day of tubing down the clear river to the 'rock pool' – a deep green swimming hole complete with massive fallen tree trunk and enormous central rock – or riding along the jungle trails, I loved watching from the hammocks hung in the bar cabana for signs of elusive animal life in the thick jungle. Wooden-floored, the bar was romantically lit by paraffin lamps at night, the only time the animals might come out. Although the owners Ray and Vicki assured us the jungle was teeming with jaguarundi, jaguars and armadillos, only the tarantulas ever graced us with their presence. I have a fear of spiders quite unrivalled in any other human being.

'Really, it's the largest we've ever seen,' said Vicki as she inspected the beautiful yet monstrous creature on *my* cabana wall.

After a few days of acclimatisation, I felt ready to venture further in, to more basic conditions – conditions which in themselves would be luxury compared to trekking through virgin jungle in Burma, pack on back, in search of love in the form of a cat. Jimmy's jungle home was on the Sibun River, off the charmingly named Hummingbird

Highway, one of Belize's three main roads. Having bravely eschewed the mundane London life of job, flat and car (or money, heating and fun, as I later came to realise), he had been living for the past seven years on government land. Unfortunately his neighbours, owners of a beautiful citrus plantation, had forgotten to tell him this, when they took $6,000 off him for it six years ago. But this was typical of Belize, Vicki and Ray had earlier told me. Ex-pats who made the country their home had to be unfazed by the lack of efficiency and ease or they never made it. Jimmy was unfazed. He had built a few houses and installed electricity. He had fought off wild animals and bathed himself in the clear waters of the Sibun River. And when he wasn't in Belize, he was working with underprivileged children in England – the man was a mixture of Jesus and Indiana Jones.

But building a house and installing electricity mean different things in different places. In the jungle a house means a stilted bed six feet up with a thatched hat, no walls and a rickety ladder. Vicki's cabanas were quite the height of elegance, I now realised. Electricity in the jungle means one bulb and music from a cassette recorder for half an hour every night.

'Oh, it's just lovely,' I trilled, horrified, when Jimmy showed us to our hut. It was 300 metres down a rugged trail away from the main kitchen hut, in which there was a table, with slanty benches, a filthy old oven and a large water tank full of brown water. The trail was a muddy line just inches wide, quite unlike the well-worn paths of

Pook's Hill. I sat gingerly on the edge of the flea-bitten mattress, whose sheets smelt of a thousand sweaty, smelly, pot-smoking teenage boys. And the lack of walls gave one a most unprotected feeling when trying to sleep. In fact the afternoon of our arrival, I tried to have a little rest, and was unable to, because some nearby creature of the jungle was taking its post-prandial nap and snoring so loudly the stilts were shaking. There was only one way to survive, I realised, and that was to be as stoned as possible.

Back at the kitchen hut I poured myself a glass of water from Jimmy's tank. It was brown.

'It's the cleanest water you're ever likely to drink,' he assured me, even though a quick peek at the roof from which rainwater dripped into the tank revealed great clumps of insects in rivulets and the odd small dead rodent. But there was no arguing with Jimmy. He was the King of the Jungle and he knew everything.

I sat down to watch Jimmy potter about. His arms were muscled from chopping logs, hauling thatch, wrestling with tigers (presumably). His trousers slipped down to reveal enough buttock to qualify as a builder. Normally this revolted me, but now I realised with lightning-bolt clarity that he could only do this because his dingdong was so big it could hold the trousers up by itself. He *was* the King of the Jungle, I thought dozily.

'I think I'll go to the loo,' I chimed, determined to put such thoughts out of my mind.

When you wanted to go to the loo, the usual thing to do, Matt explained, was go out into the jungle with a spade and dig yourself a hole. Luckily, since Matt's last visit, Jimmy had built a loo. In typical jungle fashion, however, it had no walls at all, so I sat plonked on the filthy loo seat, looking out into the jungle, praying that a tapir wouldn't choose this moment to come hurtling through and wondering how many animals were watching. (Later, when I generously offered to clean the loo seat, Jimmy looked at me as if I'd just admitted that in a moment of uncontrolled greed I'd eaten his baby sister.)

Matt was slightly shocked when, during the night, I absolutely refused to leave the hut to dig myself a hole (the loo was miles away along another trail, not even contemplatable at night), and instead preferred to hang my white bottom over the edge of the floor six feet up. No *way* was I going to risk having my bottom bitten by a tarantula as I crouched *on the ground.*

Back in bed after this undignified moment, my numerous insect bites asked for a bit of a scratch. The almost sexual pleasure to be derived from giving the mother of all mosquito bites a really good scratch was multiplied 237 times, because that's how many insect bites I had accumulated since my arrival in Belize. Haaaah. It felt good. Scratch scratch scratch. Haaaraaaagh. I scratched myself raw until my nails were brown and I could feel blood sticking to my clothes. Of course, due to the number of insects, sleeping naked under the mosquito net in the cool night air, embracing nature in a balmy star-kissed sleep, is the last thing the jungle allows. I was covered head to foot in dirty clothes and days-old knickers. Finally, grumpily, I settled down for a bit of peace.

But not quiet. The jungle at night is thumpingly loud. Because of the scuffling under the bed that heralded a rat the size of a small dog, the spiders scuttling across the floor, the branches falling and snapping, the toucans screeching to the jaguarundi chasing each other through the stilts of the hut, well rested was the last thing I was by morning. Matt of course had slept like a baby and so had Jimmy. Normally horrified by such wastrelness, at breakfast I reached gratefully for the joint, after which I felt ready for a bath.

This I knew I'd be taking at the river, so I made my way down the steep hill. It had rained during the night so the path was a slide of mud. Goody, I thought angrily. The jolt from landing on my bum made me feel as though I had dislodged a disc. At the river, I stripped off, hoping no pea-shooting natives were watching, and waded into the muddy water. Immediately thousands of insects swarmed to me. Some, the little blighters, hung on to the night's raw wounds, and wouldn't bugger off until I'd immersed myself entirely, horizontally, that is, because the water was shallow for miles.

I had to walk for 100 metres over ouch ouch, ooh, sharp pointy little stones to get to deeper water, so I wore my Nike Air Rifts as I swam (which then simply refused to dry until I was back in England). The water felt cool and fresh, but my breathing came in gasps, because of the shadows under the water that resembled vicious river monsters. They were in fact just rocks, which made themselves known by jagged cuts to the knees and shins at the last minute, too late to be avoided.

Finally at the rapids I could enjoy the deep water and sploshed about a bit, relaxed for the first time since my arrival. The rapids were noisy but cheery and I trod water for a little until I turned round to be confronted by Jimmy watching me from a rock by the water's edge.

'For God's sake, cover yourself,' I mumbled under my breath, but couldn't quite take my eyes off his dingaling. Which was bovine.

Luckily I didn't have to stare too long, as Jimmy had a brief swim and headed back because it started to rain. It was glorious and, I felt, filmic, to be rained on, a virgin ('A *what*?' shouted Matt later in disbelief, then 'Ha!' with speed and, well, venom) in this virgin jungle. The raindrops were the size of marbles; as they hit the water enormous droplets flew up to mimic them. The trees and bushes by the side of the river stretched up for miles, their greenness intensified by the deep grey of the sky.

It was all very romantic until I got back to my clothes, left out under those magical skies by the river and now soaking wet. As I crouched under a tree hoping I'd dry off, having forgotten to bring a towel, I realised that I felt sticky and entirely unclean and that my feet and ankles were covered in shit-coloured mud. I squelched my way back up to the huts, uncomfortable, cold, wet, my hair in unglamorous straggles around my ears, thinking: This place wants to *break* me.

But I soon realised that it was not the place so much as the inhabitants who got my goat.

Me: 'Gosh, the sun is so hot!'

Jimmy: 'Nah, this is nothing. Ha! You should see the dry season.'

Me: 'Aaargh! That's the largest ant I've ever seen!'

Jimmy: 'That? It's just a baby. Be nice to it.'

A lazy yet horrifyingly unrelaxed day. Finally, thankfully, it was time for bed. Unfortunately, going to bed meant my late-night trawl through the jungle to the place I called home. By the time I realised this, my imagination had done its very worst. Spiders the size of sheep crawling towards me, their jaws opening and shutting, their eyes gleaming red. Flying cockroaches hitting my face, leaving a smear of goo as they went, goo that was so thumping with poisonous germs that my immune system would never be the same again; rats the size of armadillos, scampering too fast to be caught, their scratchy nails cutting off skin as they dashed over my feet.

I turned on the only torch and threw myself along the trail through the trees, Matt's cries behind me: 'Wait! Slow down! I can't see a bloody thing.'

Next morning I tried a bath again. This time I whistled a whiffly 'Oh yes, I am almost an outdoors pro', as I attached the shower gel to a piece of string to carry around my neck. I was trying to be subtle about the bottle but just as I set off Jimmy spied it.

'You're not going to pollute the river, are you?' he snapped. I turned round.

'I am. I bloody well am. Without wishing to be callous, polluting this river is definitely going to be the highlight of my day. Mother Nature can go *fuck* herself.'

He looked hurt, and lit up his fifth joint for comfort. It was just after ten.

'Tralala, I shall be clean,' I sang loudly as I washed my hair, my ears, everything, once down at the river. It was a strange feeling indeed. Just then I heard the unmistakable pitter, pat, tip, bong bong of the world's most irritating instrument. Oh no, I thought. Jimmy's obviously got a bongo drum. And by the sounds of it, thinks he can play. However, like all white boys who get near the thing, he's *wrong. Totally* wrong.

As I hauled my clean body in dirty clothes up the hill once again, sure enough, there he was in a cloud of spliff smoke, tapping and bonging away, his head on one side as though utterly caught up in the music. If music was the right word – which it wasn't. I stomped off to the hut.

There was a huge pile of washing up to be done, which I simply did not want to do. Walking through the jungle was never that relaxing, because you had to keep an eye out, but by now I was used to the routine and knew the log I had to climb over. Just as I was thinking: This hut is miles away, am I taking the right path? it showed up ahead of me. Aaah, home. A little hut in the protective jungle.

I settled down for a snooze under the mosquito net. Five minutes later I woke up, my bottom itching horribly. I whipped down my pants and saw fifteen new white bumps sticking out from my rump. Little insects were whacking around in my pants. I flicked at them to get them off. I hit harder and harder, turning myself rapidly as I went like a cat chasing its tail, until I had flicked the final one off. I covered up quickly, the raw tails of thread from my hippie Mexican skirt adding their own brand of rubbing to the injured area. I turned round to see Jimmy smirking.

'Attracting the insects, are we?' he sneered.

'Certainly seem to be.'

I flashed an undaunted Hollywood smile pointedly at him. I held the Esther Williams gesture until he got the message and walked off into the jungle, twirling his machete, followed by his dogs.

Aah, the dogs. When the dogs (a mother and son) came to say hello, great swarms of fleas came too. You could actually see them riding the dogs' backs and hovering up like an unwelcome halo. These were the most mutty, bitten, mangey animals I had ever seen. They lived in dirt, they ate off dirt. Every bone in their skeleton was highly visible. They looked miserable. The male had a gaping pus-filled wound on its nostril, giving it gyp whenever it breathed in, i.e. every second of its miserable life. The nostril had obviously been bitten by a nasty animal (its mother perhaps) or cut on something sharp. It was red raw and made my eyes water just to look at it.

'Oh the poor things,' I said under my breath.

'Nah,' issued predictably from Jimmy's mouth. 'I've never seen them looking so healthy or happy. I've never come back before and seen them in such good condition. They have so much fun here.'

'Which will account for their "get me out of here" hangdog expressions,' I muttered.

I gingerly tickled them on the forehead, giving them a little of the much-needed affection they craved.

'Yes, my dear,' I crooned quietly. 'If you weren't a dawg, I might consider taking you home. If you were a beautiful Burmese cat, things could be very different for you. You'd live in England, where there are neither tarantulas nor deadly snakes. The weather is cooler, granted, but it's comfortable. Sort of. *Anyway*. In my large and tastefully decorated home, which borders on the sumptuous if you use your imagination, you'd eat at table with me. Imagine sushi eel or fresh grilled chicken or fried steak. You'd be brushed regularly and tended to by the vet. You'd sleep in my soft, clean –'

'Oh will you cut that out?' broke in Jimmy, rudely is the only suitable adverb. 'Stop winding yourself and the dogs up.'

I looked at the dogs and sure enough they were wagging their tails in unison, looking up hopefully as if to say, 'Come on. Extend your rules just once. We can be very catlike if you would just use *your* imagination.'

There was one moment of peace. Jimmy was a surprisingly good cook. That night he served up barbecued chicken breasts, vinaigretted salad and white rice. The chicken was soft and long trails of barbecue juice ran down my chin. The dogs had been somewhat near the barbecue but I didn't let this thought bother me. The salad could never have been washed considering Jimmy's dislike of changing the washing-up water even when it was black with dirt, but that was not a problem either. The plates still had remnants of yesterday's meal on them but I let that pass as well.

After supper while we were relaxing with a spliff, we talked. Conversation with Jimmy was usually a frustrating affair.

Me: 'So do you build your huts alone?'

Jimmy: 'Sometimes I work alone and sometimes the guys help me.'

Me: 'Which guys?'

Jimmy: 'These guys I know . . .'

Me: 'And is the process quick?'

Jimmy: 'Sometimes it's quick, sometimes it's slow.'

In my mind: 'Who do you think you are? The Dalai bleedin' Lama?'

But that night we were actually having a laugh. However, our moment of *bonhomie* was shattered by Jimmy's own woodwork. My back was resting against the slanting wooden board that Jimmy called a back rest, but which, seconds after the punch-line delivery, slid itself free from the nail it rested on to swing gently in the breeze. As it did this I wumped spectacularly to the floor, scattering midges, ants and cockroaches with my descent, even squashing a few, I'm happy, albeit crippled, to say. Jimmy didn't help me up, because that would have been the reaction of a gentleman (nor did Matt, mind you, he just laughed until he was doubled up).

This triggered pent-up rage which issued forth like volcanic venom and the long-awaited showdown presented itself at the door, dressed in a matador's cloak uttering 'Ta-da'. Simultaneously the dreams I had secretly harboured about living The Good Life, with tamed jaguars scampering at my feet, and love and lust under the starry canopy, slipped out under the Showdown's feet.

'Oh you bongo-playing ganja-smoking *idiot*,' I scream.

'You're just jungle-incompatible,' he said, as though this weren't something to be proud of.

'If by that you mean I'm not a filthy pig whose mattresses are covered in fleas, whose nails are more dirt than tip, whose sheets stink from so many druggy hippie soiled boys' bodies in between, then yes, yes, I suppose I am jungle-incompatible,' I whispered savagely. 'I am out of here. *Matt!* Tomorrow, first thing, we're going. I don't care if I have to walk back to Belize City, we are *outtahere*.'

I had managed two days.

Matt said that he obliged because he could see the finger of blame starting to point at him, which was his excuse for air-lifting me out to the nearest five-star hotel. When we checked in and I ran a bath, I was delirious with joy, ecstatic and extreme in my reaction, singing, shrieking, running around naked. Matt asked reception if they had any Valium. I still claim however that he was grateful for the reaction, being a creature of comfort himself. Especially as I then spent £80 getting everything we owned laundered, so that not a blade, not a drop, not a whisker of the jungle would return with us to England.

Because of memories like these, it is no comfort whatso-ever to hear Matt telling me that various parts of Burma and Thailand are covered in jungle. Yes, in many ways jungles are misconceived as romantic places where one can gape in wonder at nature. It is dangerous to gape in a place where insects the size of humming-birds can fly into one's mouth. It is naive to think one can only live a spiritually and other-wise fulfilled life if one returns to nature, a concept fed to me by films such as *Dancing With Wolves* and *Greystoke*.

But on the other hand Cindy Crawford, and many others, pay thousands to attend wilderness therapies in California, the theory being that when faced with nature to an extreme the trivialities of life fall away, leaving the real issues bare. If she can wake up at six, do yoga twice a day and hike for six hours on little food in order to overcome her inner fears then surely I can battle it out with the mosquitoes and jungle to find my cat? Yes! I will prevail! My fighting spirit, slightly sozzled, resurrects itself from the pits of my empty wine glass and thumps its hand triumphantly on the table. Or alternatively I could avoid the jungle, it mopes, lowering itself gingerly back into my body in 192, where it is confronted by Matt, looking wonderful. Unfortunately he then opens his mouth.

At midnight I am on the paper-littered Portobello Road, wending my way home, the smell of rotten fruit and veg gently tingeing the air. Narrowly avoiding a shuffling, dishevelled female tramp muttering, 'Oooh I've had a day of it – emotional battles with astral warlords,' I weigh up the attractions of glamorous tête-à-têtes such as these and a strange caper through Burma and Thailand alone until I make it back to my dark, empty, catless flat. I climb gratefully into my comfortable bed only to be tortured by a cold hot-water bottle. This adds to the irritation I feel at Matt's words, which have unsettled me and shaken my confidence in my project.

Why do I not feel whole unless I have a cat? Because two years ago I set off on a road trip around America with my beloved brown Burmese cat, Claudius. I returned alone because he died, which he did this day one year ago in America. In total he was with me for almost twenty years of my life, witness to the event I felt made me a woman: the loss of my virginity and the one that really did: the death of my mother.

We went slightly bonkers in the States. We visited a celebrity pet-hairstylist. We got chased by a bear in the Appalachian Mountains. And then a Park Ranger – that's a person, not a car – much more scary. We rode with psychic cowboys in Texas. We hiked the Grand Canyon. And then he got fined for being a cat. (I paid.) I gambled someone else's money away in Vegas and he was my alibi out of there. I wore a lot of silly clothes. I was neurotic, he was Zen. (That's because he never drove the car or carried any bags.) He was a huge part of my life.

'You might learn to love humans,' my sister said when I was back in London.

'Oh do belt *up*,' I replied. 'Don't be such a *bore*.'

Claudius and I had known each other for so long – we'd listened to each other breathe in sleep night after night, we knew each other's reactions and moods. I felt completely comfortable with him, something I'd never felt with any of my boyfriends. Claudius and I – apart from his midnight mousing escapades – had the same life.

When he died, I lost intimacy, understanding, comfort. That's what I want to replace.

The world is divided into two: those who love their pets and those who consider pet-lovers to be emotionally inadequate. Feeling the auspices of memory turning my gills slightly yellow, I rummage under my bed for my favourite childhood book, *Orlando the Marmalade Cat.* Ah, the halcyon days of Claudius. When he was around I was never emotionally over-involved with random people, because he provided so much security, and automatically disliked anyone unsuitable.

Jungle or no, finding a feline outlet for my love is definitely the way to go. I must get another cat and call it Claudius in memory of the first. In fact, every cat I have from now on shall be called Claudius. Even if it's a female. Yes, the patter of four tiny feet would do me so much good.

Next evening, drinking in Woody's with Sylvie, my best friend, I am explaining my plan, my doubts, my fears. I love Sylvie because she thinks she's Elvis reincarnated, in spite of the fact that their lives overlapped by seven years. She even once tried to get a job as an Elvis impersonator, and kicked up a fuss when she was turned down on account of being a woman. Once on an overnight train from Paris to Rome during her year off, she went to the bathroom to wash her teeth only to return and find the train had split, leaving her bags, money and passport in one part of the train and herself in just a nightie in the other.

There's one thing I don't like about her, though. Her attitude to animals is dodgy. She bought a Dalmatian a couple of years back after the Walt Disney film came out, and in her fur-throated Maxfield Parrish coat promenaded the dog around London. Then suddenly she had the Dalmatian put down.

'Cancer,' she sniffed dismissively.

In such a young dog? I sobbed when told.

However, when removing his bowl and basket, Conchita, our mutual cleaner, also found three recently chewed Prada handbags. Mystery solved.

'My one fear is that I might not be able to love another cat. Claudius was so exceptional that another might just be an ugly moggie, a pale imitation, in comparison with him.'

'Well, why not avoid the competition with Claudius and go the other way? Get yourself a moggie! One that is a stray in the street and chooses *you* so then you know you're spiritual partners in life?'

(Excuse Sylvie. In spite of her penchant for Prada, she's an out-and-out hippie.)

'Don't be *ridiculous*, Sylv. I can't possibly get a *moggie*. Anyway, Burmese and Siamese cats are the only breeds that travel. Siamese even sit on your shoulder when you walk. You know I need to be free and un-tied down.'

'But, Clare, why go all the way to Burma and Siam to do it? Why don't you just get a Siamese cat over here?'

Silence as the world newly dawns.

'That is a *fantastic* idea,' I reply. 'It hadn't even occurred to me.'

Which is true. This would solve the problem of the jungle.

Next I visit Mrs Westford-Norton's litter of Siamese kittens in Hampshire. I park next to her Land-Rover which sports a sticker saying 'Hunting's Natural. Foxes do it too!'. She leads me through a chintzy drawing room to a cat room with a warm box full of two-month-old kittens. Apart from their inherent fluffy innocence, they are scrawny, skinny nightmares, with tails like string, noses like Concorde and ears that hit the ceiling. Their tiny bodies are almost too thin and long for their skeletons to support them. They look like Yoda from *Star Wars*. I don't bond with any of them. Inbred and overbred, they are too nervous to live the robust exciting life I have in store for us. I want a cat like Claudius, muscly, chunky, good to hold and cuddle, not a bundle of bones.

'Yes, they're delicate little things,' says Mrs W-N. 'But perfect pedigree, exactly as the Siamese Cat Joint Advisory Committee drew up in 1980. Their points are perfect.'

'But they look rather nervous.'

They have all started an ear-splitting miaow, trademark of the Siamese cat.

'Well, they're moderns, you see.'

'Didn't they used to be chunkier than this?'

'You're thinking of the Classic, which is less refined than this and came about in the late seventies, when they started to breed out the trademark squint and kinked tail. Then of course there is the Traditional – or the Applehead as it's known – which is how the breed was a hundred years ago.'

'Ah yes! Perhaps that's what I'm looking for.'

'Well, good luck,' she harrumphs. 'Because there aren't any in England.'

But I am not to be thwarted. Every great project has a few stumbling blocks to test your mettle. Or is it metal? Did Hannibal cross the Alps in balmy sunshine? I think not. Did Josephine let the stink of garlic and a stocky appearance blister her great love for Napoleon? Of course not. Did . . . oh you get my drift.

After phoning the President of the Traditional Siamese Cat Association in Jersey, I realise that some sort of war is being waged between the breeders: those that follow the 1980 list of new points, that created the Modern, and those that love the traditional, believing that the Moderns are unhealthy creatures akin to overbred bulldogs that can't whelp, ultra Pekinese with breathing and eye problems and elongated dachshunds whose overworked spines eventually lead to paralysis.

'Apparently the first owner in England was Lilian Velvey,' Sheelagh le Cocq tells me, 'whose brother Owen Gould had been given them for her by their brother Edward Gould, the Acting Vice-Consul to Siam. The story goes that King Chulalongkorn, the son of the King of Siam made famous by the musical *The King and I*, offered him anything he liked from the palace when he called to bid farewell. When he asked for a pair of the Siamese cats, the King was upset but honoured his promise. It's not definite that this story is true, but many Siamese-lovers like to believe that a hundred years ago you couldn't get a Siamese out of the country without the King's permission and that they were bred specifically for the palace in Bangkok.'

Sheelagh advises me I will have to look abroad for a traditional Siamese cat and gives me the number of a breeder in France.

'*Ah oui, bonjour, Madame. Je m'appelle Clare et je cherche un chat, traditionnel, siamois . . .*'

'*Bah oui, mais le problème c'est . . .*' after which an interminably long flurry of French, that simultaneously makes me panic and feel irritated that after a degree in the language I can't understand a word.

I think the gist is that she doesn't have any. This after several typically Franco-Anglo exchanges in which I manage to insult her horribly. When she says she might have some kittens in the near future, I remark, '*Que ça c'est excitant!*' which roughly means, 'You're really turning me on.' Equally, while taking down her name and address, and trying to spell 'q' in French, I hope she doesn't take my remark, '*Vous avez un cul dans votre nom*?' literally, as in, 'You have an arse in your name?'

After several calls all over Europe, it becomes clear that my original idea of Thailand is not quite so far-fetched after all. And that a thorough search through the royal cities might be a good place to start.

As for Burmese cats, the soft-voiced Mrs Buxton of the Burmese Cat Club uses words like 'fruitful' and 'nourishing' in relation to my plan, and only slightly skewers the whole thing with the news that the cats in Burma are Birman and not Burmese.

'Birmans have long hair, blue eyes and Siamese-type markings, but their most distinguishing feature is that the toes on all four feet are white, whereas Burmese have short hair, traditionally are brown and have golden-yellow eyes. They're two quite different breeds of cat.'

Burmese, like Siamese, are mentioned in the Ancient Thai Cat Book (written in the Ayutthaya period between 1350 and 1767).

'Brown cats,' she continues, 'thought to be another strain of Siamese, were more highly prized in Burma than Siam and considered sacred.'

They were therefore only kept by kings and high priests and lived in temples and palaces. Each cat had its own servant, there to ensure it was never stolen and never bred any moggies. The servant would be harshly punished if any harm came to the cat. The cats were given very occasionally to someone exceptional as an honour of the highest kind.

Burmese cats were first introduced to the West in 1930 by Dr Joseph C. Thompson, a geneticist from San Francisco who acquired a female named Wong Mau. Dr Thompson was at one time a Buddhist monk in a Lama monastery in Tibet. As well as breeding cats, he practised psychiatry from his bungalow in San Francisco. Part of his therapy included giving his patients a pregnant Siamese cat, the idea being that once they had raised a litter of lovely kittens, they would have forgotten about their problems. In fact Wong Mau sat by him as he carried out his psychiatric consultations.

She was considered a dark Siamese by the American Cat Fanciers. Dr Thompson felt her markings were very different from the Siamese and tried to create a breeding programme to isolate Wong Mau's Burmese traits.

The Burmese was introduced to Britain by Sydney and Lilian France of Derby. Lilian caused much excitement when her cat Casa Gatos da Foong made his debut at the Croydon Cat Club show at Lime Grove Baths, Hammersmith, in November 1949. If nothing else, she proved that Burmese cats, along with Siamese, are the owners of extravagantly aristocratic names.

Mrs Buxton finishes by saying that she has never been to Burma, but believes that there are plenty of Burmese cats in Thailand, going under their Thai name of the Copper Cat.

★　　★　　★

With an idea of the history of these kingly cats under my belt, I feel more and more convinced that finding them at their source in the royal cities of Burma and Thailand is the only way to go. And frankly I can't face any more evenings in Notting Hill watering spots, with competitive chippy clones whose idea of friendship is to put one down repeatedly. I need to get out and breathe some fresh unEnglish air.

Now what about good contacts? Actually the only Burman I know is my neighbour Wayne, a retired builder, who is very knowledgeable about potted plants. As for the language, the only words I understand are '*Kanà kanà andeh*', which mean 'I vomit often'.

In spite of these minor inconveniences (no language, no friends), I am simultaneously equipping myself with mosquito repellent in the local chemist and confusedly staring at row upon row of shampoo and conditioner, unable to choose, when I am struck by the ridiculousness of packing all the usual holiday-style junk. Aren't I going to a Buddhist country? Didn't King Anawrahta introduce Buddhism to Burma after defeating the neighbouring Buddhist Mon king in 1057 and incorporating much Mon culture into Burma (or Bamar as it was then known)? Wouldn't it make more sense to try and absorb some of the country's customs from the moment of arrival – hit the ground running as it were? After all, in America, my battle with all things consumerist was not quite successful.

Then and there I decide to adopt a new Buddhist

philosophy, whereby all things Gucci are no longer sacrosanct. Gone will be the need for my accountant to shout at me when I put £195 shoes under 'equipment' in my accounts. Quick research reveals that trainee Buddhist monks are allowed the following: three pieces of cloth, a mat, a bowl, a blade, a water strainer and a needle.

Not quite able to cut down to that extent, I pack:

Three pieces of cloth (linen trousers, pink cotton shirt, blue skirt)
Mat (one of those camping sleeping-bag sheets)
Notebook
Books (including one guide)
Torch
Camera
Two bottles of Body Shop travelwash
Toothbrush
Toothpaste
Mascara
Medicine

I also include in my rucksack copious amounts of pens and lipsticks, as presents to give away. But that is all – although there is one luxury in there. Can you spot it? The toothpaste. I've recently formed the ugly habit of spending £10 on some herbal concoction that promises to keep my teeth white. Which I think will be useful in a country where everyone chews betel – areca-nut wrapped in green betel leaves smeared with lime paste that stains the teeth red and eventually black.

Having packed my tiny rucksack, all that remains is to say goodbye to my friends.

TWO

STILL LONDON

WHEN I TELL my friends that the time has come to stop making their lives hell and to get another cat, everyone, to a T, is thrilled. When I explain that I am in fact going to Burma to get another Burmese their jaws drop a little. But not Camilla's. Camilla, being a honking Sloane, thinks it all very jolly.

'Oh but you must meet the next King of Burma!' she barks down the phone.

'Darling! But I'd love to!' I bark back. 'Where does he live?'

'Notting Hill!'

Of course. Silly me, to think anyone should live any-where but Notting Hill. More than anything this confirms the need to get out. She gives me his mobile phone number and I call him.

'This is the King of Burma,' he answers.

I introduce myself, explain that I might be going to Burma and ask if we can talk. He says of course, let's meet at the Anna Hotel in Bayswater at 9.30 p.m. on Friday week. We can talk there without fear of being heard.

This is not the first time I have learnt of the need for

secrecy where Burma is concerned. The military dictatorship has bred paranoia into every Burmese heart. The
guidebooks say that in Burma the people risk questioning
and perhaps even imprisonment if they are seen talking to
foreigners, and that's if you are lucky enough to get into
the country in the first place.

In the meantime I get my shots.

As the doctor injects a rabies dose into my arm, she
quietly murmurs, 'Now be absolutely sure not to touch
any dogs or cats.'

'No *cats*?'

'No.'

'Er, not even cats?' I ask.

'*No*. Even if they don't look rabid they could carry
rabies. A girl died in America recently after playing with
a puppy. There was nothing the doctors could do for her.
They even injected her in the brain and she still died.'

Aargh.

While waiting for my appointment with the King the
following Friday, I decide to mug up a little on Burmese
history so as not to come over as a half-wit when I meet
him. My potted version:

For centuries Burma was ruled by a string of despotic
monarchs, whose power was unquestioningly accepted
by the people. On his accession, the last Burmese king,
Thibaw, followed the example of many of his forebears,
and murdered any other pretenders, i.e. the majority of
his family. There was an intense massacre in February

1879 when almost one hundred royals were slaughtered, including Thibaw's brothers, their wives, sisters and children. (There were plenty of them, for Thibaw's father, the recently deceased King Mindon, had seventy sons by different wives. In fact Suhpayalat, Thibaw's wife, was one of the daughters of Mindon's main queen, which, according to my maths, means Thibaw married his half-sister.) One of the favourite slaughter methods used by earlier Burmese kings was to put the offending royal in a red velvet sack and then beat them to death. That way you couldn't see the blood.

After a few Anglo–Burmese wars, based on trading interests on the Indian border, the British deposed Thibaw and his wife on 29 November 1885. They went to India. Although their kings had not created massive empires, the Burmese had for centuries enjoyed a seemingly indomitable monarchy and accompanying strong self-image. The monarchy had done precious little to improve their lives, but the Burmese were far from gruntled to see Thibaw led from Mandalay Palace to permanent exile. They were psychologically unprepared for the Brits, who treated Burma as an extension of India, rather than a separate entity. Because the British didn't take into consideration Burma's customs and way of life and imposed their own concept of education and government, relations between the British and the Burmese were sometimes a tad strained. So the Burmese soon became interested in nationalism.

Aung San became prominent in 1936 when, as editor of the Student Union's magazine at Rangoon University, he refused to name the author of an article that criticised a university official. His subsequent expulsion and the consequent student strike were highly publicised. He was reinstated and by 1938 was both a popular figure and head of the Rangoon University Student Union and the All Burma Student Union.

During the Second World War, Aung San escaped to Japan, to campaign for arms to support an uprising against the British in the battle for independence. He and 'Thirty Comrades' formed the basis of the future Burmese Independence Army. He became known as Bogyoke – General. At the end of 1941, together with the Japanese army who promised them independence, the BIA invaded Burma and expelled the British. But then in a dastardly imperial double cross, the Japanese refused to grant independence – and gave the Burmese a brutal thumping to prove it. Aung San then defeated the Japanese, with help, ironically, from the Allies he had just fought so hard to expel. Still Aung San had to fight for two more years to achieve the Aung San–Attlee agreement of 1946 in London which planned for the transfer of British power to an independent Burmese government. The Burmese adored their hero but Aung San was assassinated on 19 July 1948.

Burma became independent on 4 January 1948. For the next fourteen years, the economic and political situation in the country was shaky. U Nu, the Prime Minister, handed over the reins of power in 1958 to a military government headed by General Ne Win, one of Aung San's original 'Thirty Comrades'. Ne Win means 'Brilliant Like the Sun' and is the modest *nom de guerre* he awarded himself. In 1960 U Nu came back to power, but in 1962, after more political turmoil, Ne Win staged a military coup and abolished the parliament. The situation then nosedived. He took over all businesses, demonetised large banknotes without compensation, and drove out all foreigners. He isolated the country from the rest of the world. Burma quickly became one of the world's poorest countries.

Since then, the economy, through ignorance, misman-agement and personal greed, has been slowly strangled. Rights to mine Burma's substantial natural resources (jade, rubies, oil) have been sold to neighbouring countries to line the pockets of the few. So many teak forests have been cleared by the Thais that the land now faces serious ecological problems with deforestation and dust bowls. But it gets worse: Ne Win's arrogant rule has been one of complete repression. He makes Stalin look like a pussy cat.

In July 1988 a student in a Rangoon teashop was attacked by the son of the chairman of the local People's Council, who was subsequently released from detention unpun-ished. This ignited a massive public reaction against the government's high-handed treatment of the people. Fed up with Ne Win's military dictatorship, the people staged demonstrations asking for an end to the one-party rule.

The government responded by gunning down the dem-onstrators, including students, children, women and monks. Still the demonstrations continued. Ne Win resigned, but his replacement, Sein Lwin, known as the Butcher, was hated by the people, as was the next replacement. And people believed Ne Win was still in control anyway. The demonstrations continued for about six weeks, but during this time around 3,000 people were killed, and many thousands more arrested, imprisoned and tortured. At one point forty-one people suffocated to death in a police van. The government never accepted responsibility for these deaths and vastly underestimated the number of people killed elsewhere.

Finally the birth of SLORC was announced (the State Law and Order Restoration Council) whose very name suggests the drain it was to become on people's lives. (It later changed its name to the SPDC – the State Peace and Development Council. Oh and it also changed the name of the country from Burma to Myanmar.) SLORC was really just another incarnation of the existing government, with elections promised for May 1989.

It was around this time that Aung San Suu Kyi, Aung San's charismatic daughter, came into the public eye. When the demonstrations started she was in Rangoon nursing her mother who had suffered a stroke. Previously she was living in England with her British husband, Michael Aris. She headed the National League for Democracy, campaigned around the country and was soon so immensely popular that in July 1989 she was put under house arrest. In 1990 she was awarded the Nobel Peace Prize for her non-violent stance against the government. Having declared Aung San Suu Kyi unfit to run for office (er, she was married to a foreigner and had lived abroad), the government allowed free elections for the first time in thirty years.

The NLD won 392 of the 485 seats. Of course the government then refused to allow the NLD to assume power, claiming a state-approved constitution had to be passed first, which to this day has not happened. Many members of the NLD, including all the major leaders, were then imprisoned, exiled or killed. Aung San Suu Kyi was released from her house arrest in July 1995 but is not allowed out of Rangoon – except for permanent exile.

During the 1997 Visit Myanmar Year, she advocated a travel-boycott policy, saying that money from tourists helped support the military government. Afraid she would not be let back in the country were she to leave, Aung San Suu Kyi decided to stay in Burma when she heard her husband was dying of cancer. In his turn, Michael Aris was refused a visa to visit her for the last time. She made the ultimate personal sacrifice for what she believed in.

After reading as much as I can about Burma, I feel terrible. Suddenly my desire for a lovely Burmese kitten seems completely out of place in the context of a country riddled with fear and repression. And a king claiming rights to a long-lost throne equally spurious. So when I arrive at the highly unswish Anna Hotel and am confronted with the shabby seventies décor, the dirty once-white walls, the thin carpets, the half-finished lavatories, the intense seediness of it all, I don't know what to think. But deposed royals can't always stay at the Savoy, I realise. I must keep my mind open.

The King stands in the bar area. He is a small unprepossessing man of slight build, wearing fragile-looking specs. Next to him is his right-hand man, taller and stouter with white hair and a navy pinstripe suit. He has the most enormous stye on his eye and orders glasses of red plonk in an 'I say, old chaps' voice.

Our first topic is the Royal Burma Society, of which the King is the president. Founded in 1993, its objectives are to promote friendship between Britain and Burma, to encourage travel there, to inform the British about the true state of Burmese culture, heritage and history, and to alleviate the suffering of the very poor Burmese in Thailand.

'The group is mainly made up of foreigners who are interested in Burma,' says the King.

'And those who are interested in restoring the monarchy to the throne,' says his friend.

Aung San Suu Kyi in *Freedom from Fear* wrote:

There had not been much cause for the people to love the monarchy in the past – the king in his golden palace had simply been a symbol of power and glory of their race. Now that the glory was extinguished, the Burmese were too canny to wish the power to go back into autocratic hands if they could help it.

She was referring to an incident in 1930 when Hsaya San, also presenting himself as a future monarch, had led a peasants' rebellion against the British. (Unfortunately his followers' belief in swords and magic amulets had done little against the gun-power of the British.)

'The group also hopes to deblacken the generals' reputation in Burma. There is a world conspiracy to make them seem worse than they are.'

'Really?'

'Burma needs its king back on the throne,' says the friend, gazing lovingly at his ticket to pseudo-sophistication. I had to bite my tongue.

'So how does the group try to achieve this?' I say, not entirely sure how a king is currently more important than democracy.

'We hold social events, black-tie balls and such.'

'Very useful. When did you leave Burma?'

The King left Burma in 1961 and has not been back since. If the government allows, he might soon boat up the Irrawaddy River from Pagan to Mandalay, but he'll have to keep a low profile.

'There might be security problems, if people see me, there might be demonstrations, wanting me to lead them . . .'

'Really. You think they'd remember you?'

'Absolutely. The Burmese people know that a boy left their country.'

He mentions poems that speak of a Minlaung Saviour, a prince who will appear and save the nation.

'The notion is in the heart of every Burmese person. Except the politicians.'

'But what about the NLD? Why couldn't they save Burma?'

'The NLD is not very effective,' he says. 'It is led by Mrs Michael Aris.'

Aung San Suu Kyi, or the Lady as she is sometimes known, is the leading light, perhaps the only light, of hope in Burma.

'You see, Mrs Michael Aris has . . .'

He refers to her a couple more times in this way.

'Why do you insist on calling her by her husband's name?' I interrupt, somewhat irritated.

'Because that's her name,' he replies.

'In the same way if you were married to me you'd be Mrs So and So,' says So and So.

I look at his stye.

'But she has her own name,' I reply.

'She never lived in Burma. She lived in Oxford. She should take her husband's name.'

Ignoring the chauvinist garbage, I cut to the chase.

'So which would you prefer? The present government or a democracy?'

'Democracy works if the people are competent and democratic institutions are in place. But it would not be workable at this stage, as the people are not used to it. Neither the military nor the politicians have competency in running a democratic society.'

'So how would you run the country?' I ask, just supposing for a moment that we indulge in your fantasy that you're ever going to become king.

'I will run the country more hands-on than a constitutional monarch. I'll monitor the work of the government. The present generals are doing a good job in terms of national security. When I rule they would join the house of lords with the Karen and Shan feudal lords.'

Although at this point he breaks off to state that the Sawbwas, as these princes were referred to, were not *real* princes, but more like tax collectors for the king.

'They don't have standing armies, for instance,' he points out.

I wonder if we have suddenly been transported to the Middle Ages. A millennium of political development seems to have completely bypassed him.

When I ask about his family, things suddenly become very confused.

'My family line comes from the ninth century, the Bagan line. My mother's side was from the third empire. My father's line is from the first empire, and my maternal grandfather is from the second empire.'

So. His mother is from the third empire and yet her father is from the second empire.

When I mention Thibaw and ask his connection, the King scoffs.

'Thibaw is rubbish. His mother had an affair with a monk – and Thibaw was the product of the liaison.'

It is correct that Thibaw's claim to the throne was weak in comparison with other princes, but he then goes on to say, 'According to the history books they butchered the proper royals in 1879 but it suited the British to distort the truth.'

'To what end, though?'

'History is written by the victors in every conflict. The British have lied throughout history.'

His friend harrumphs and agrees with this.

'The British are not interested in the truth,' continues the King.

They remind me of the Burmese press which, after the 1988 massacre, printed in *Working People's Daily* the words, 'The BBC . . . never tells the truth . . . It takes every opportunity to spread false news.'

'But they are good at administration,' the King adds morosely. 'The official British line is that Thibaw was the last Burmese king and that the Burmese monarchy was abolished when he went. But I own the peacock emblem. I know what the royal emblem looks like. When I release it I'll put my face on it and enlarge it so they can't copy it.'

His friend ho-ho-hos this.

I don't bother to mention that R. Shaw, the then British resident in Mandalay, had written to Colonel Horace Browne, a former resident, at the time of the 1879 massacres. Browne later noted in his diary that Mr Shaw had expressed 'his horror . . . and entreated ministers to intervene to save the survivors'. But he was effectively told by these ministers to mind his own business and that as an independent country Burma was allowed to act according to its custom. In fact many other kings before Thibaw had slaughtered their families to confirm their access to the throne (Bagan Min executed 6,000 possible pretenders in the first two years of his reign) but because of Thibaw's tenuous claim to the throne, the massacres had been particularly thorough and nasty. So I wonder how the King has a claim. Could he be one of the survivors, if there were any? Some princes were spirited away to India, including a Prince Nyoung Yan and his brother. Was he related to them?

'I never met my grandfather. It was never explained to me how he died. I did not know the names of my grandparents.'

This is a far cry from the English royal family, who know their lineage back to when first the fish started swimming and the birds a-tweeting. But apparently his great uncle was good friends with U Nu (the prime minister who inadvertently gave Ne Win his first taste of power). Apparently they sent the King to England to study British–government methods, which, if his spiel about standing armies and feudal lords is anything to go by, wasn't that successful.

We then move on to his education.

'I was privately tutored. When I was young I met Churchill and Attlee. I knew their sentiments. I was six years ahead of my contemporaries. I could have gone to medical military school in Maymio [the hill town north of Mandalay popular with the colonials, now known as Pyin U Lwin] at thirteen and would have been a qualified doctor at nineteen, but I was more interested in law.'

He did not do A levels, but went to a college in Glasgow.

Then he worked for Denis Brothers, the Irrawaddy Flotilla company, where they trained him in Dunbarton and he learnt technical drawing. He spent four years doing a sandwich course at Middlesex University, or was it polytechnic? But actually he wanted to go to Cambridge. When in 1962 the military took over, the embassy in England turned against him. He applied to Cambridge but had to stay at Middlesex otherwise the embassy wouldn't support him. He then went to Birmingham to do a Master's in thermodynamics.

Then in 1968 he was sent back to Burma to be a junior minister but he jumped planes in Frankfurt and disappeared for twenty years.

'Oh I had the most marvellous time in those twenty years,' he says. 'Such fun, such fun. I lived in absolute anonymity.'

'What, a bit like now then? So what was life like in Burma?'

'I had a wonderful life,' he replies, his eyes glazing over at the memories. 'Everywhere I go, invitations to dinner, like walking on rose petals. I experienced paradise in Burma. I believe I can get it back. If you had a wonderful childhood it gives you the strength. It makes you charitable and magnanimous and optimistic. The down side is that people take advantage of you because you're too generous. Another glass of wine please.'

The King refuses to condemn the military – a wise move as the Burmese in Britain must be careful not to make trouble for their families back home – and then claims that he has been modifying their behaviour for the last ten years.

'How?'

'I've been writing letters to them about sovereignty, about the importance of history, where they went wrong with socialism. I've sent them letters asking them to be softer in their approach.

'In 1990 I wrote a letter outlining six points of recommendation, one was to welcome back the students and open arms to the exiles from abroad. They did these things.'

Indeed the government did welcome back the students who fled to the jungles and Thailand after the 1988 uprising – if torture and imprisonment is your definition of welcome.

'They got rid of socialism after my letters.'

My jaw drops to my knees.

'But the generals seem to have lined their own pockets . . .'

'Burma is a faraway place. The generals are paid £10 a month. They do not have European bank accounts. They're poor. They work very hard. Very long hours. Yes, one general was under arrest for being like a feudal lord. That happens at lower levels when they feather their own nests. But they do not become mega rich. It's not like Nigeria. Burma is selling licences to foreign countries to exploit their natural resources, but they're not feathering their own nests by doing it themselves.'

'Oh right. Well, that's all right then.'

'But rubies are not comparable to oil. They're not that

significant. The generals have big houses and cars and servants but as for our generals living like tin gods, no they're not. I don't believe that. But the generals don't like power. People make the assumption they like power. They have to assume power. If they vacate the office, that will destabilise the country. The state will collapse. They believe democracy should arrive but they don't have the means to make it work.

'You see, I am dealing with the fourth ambassador now. The second ambassador, Tin Hlaing, I liked, he was trained by the RAF. I could speak with him any time. If he was there he would take my call. The third ambassador was U Win Aung — a foreign minister. He invited me to a secret lunch at a Japanese restaurant in Baker Street. We had a one-and-a-half-hour discussion where we bridged the gap between Downing Street and the Burmese government. I got on well with John Major's government. I used to attend the Conservative government winter balls. But since Labour got in I've not bothered to contact them. U Win Aung wanted to use me and take the credit for a good job. I'll not be recognised for the work I've done for Burma or Britain.'

'And so what do you think about the renaming of Burma?'

His friend pipes up. 'Yes, there are lots of names for lots of places. For instance, some French people call England "Angleterre", which is wrong.'

'Er, but, erm, well, that *is* the French for England.'

'Well, it's just playing with names, isn't it? There are lots of different names. Your Majesty, another drink?'

Then the King moves on to the subject of the Karens, who have been fighting for separatism from the Burmese government for forty years. Abandoned by the British during the war, the guerrilla leaders still hold out hope that the British will help them once again.

'They're not fighting for democracy but for a separate state. But the majority of Karens do not want a separate state. Anyway they can't have a separate state. It's *my* kingdom.'

His wish to speak in a private room clearly evaporated some time ago. Now people wander in and out of the bar staring.

'The Burmese are not cruel to ethnic minorities. The concept of ethnic minorities does not exist in the Burmese psyche. The differences are not discernible.'

'Mmm. That's interesting. I wonder then why Amnesty International went to such trouble to write their 1988 report on extrajudicial execution and torture of members of ethnic minorities in Burma?'

'Aung San Suu Kyi has a duty to create a cohesive Burmese society where all people are equal under the law and should join hands to create progress, not to create separatism.'

'And do you believe *you* are equal?'

'Of course I believe I'm equal. Yes. But I have bigger duties and responsibilities. If anything I am a higher servant.'

'You're like the Pope,' says his friend.

'The Royal Family supports me. Princess Anne went to Burma in 1974 and I met her recently. She was very perceptive. About a year ago she was going through a bad time. I wrote a letter supporting her. Her secretary sent me a letter back supporting me. They're very nice. She has a standing invitation to the Royal Palace in Mandalay.'

'But doesn't the palace belong to the government?'

'Downing Street always acknowledged my letters. If you want to know more about Burma, don't read the history books. They're written by academics who don't know the truth.'

'Right.'

'A lot of Burmese people see me as their king.'

'So when are you going to be crowned?'

'Next year in 2001. That is the real new Millennium. It'll take place in Germany or the Czech Republic. I have an honorary family in Bavaria. They're the family I never had. My parents passed away in the seventies. Our letters were censored and we just lost touch. But Princess Angela has a big castle there and she comes from a large dynasty. They were the bankers for the holy Roman emperors. She opened this ball recently where sixty per cent of the guests were German aristocrats. Oh we had three wonderful days of dancing. And Buzz Aldrin. Do you know him?'

'Not personally . . .'

'He's a friend of mine. I'm very well connected globally. Better than the generals.'

He leans back and smiles at a spot about a foot above my head.

Well, I think, walking away along the Bayswater Road. If the government has kept him off the throne, frankly it's the only sensible thing they've done in the past forty years. Of course I don't know whether he really is royal. However, the Burmese royals *were* thought to be a few sandwiches short of a picnic. As Harriet O'Brien states in her book *Forgotten Land*: 'Insanity resulting from years of inbreeding became a regal problem.'

A friend suggests I speak with a Burmese friend of hers, who was a guerrilla fighter in the jungle. When I phone him he suggests the Ritz for tea – not the most guerrillaish of places.

In walks a slight, lithe, elegant man, immaculately dressed in a cream linen Italian suit and soft brown-honey-coloured Gucci loafers. His skin is a beautiful *café au lait*. We order tea, which costs about a million pounds. He crosses his legs carefully and gently leans back, his arms resting delicately on the arms of his chair. If everyone in Burma is as feline as this man, I'm going to love them. After a protracted talk about London, Paris, the opera and fashion, we finally get round to Burma.

'Do you know of the King of Burma?'

'I've heard of him. A friend met him at a party and talked to him in Burmese and he scuttled away. The general theory is that he's full of rubbish. He may have royal connections but the Burmese don't want a king.'

'Will you ever go back to Burma?'

'Oh I couldn't possibly,' he says languidly. 'You see, I was fighting with the guerrillas in the jungle. The generals would eat me up for breakfast if I so much as set foot anywhere near the place.'

'And what is Ne Win like?'

'Ne Win? Oh! Your average dictator. Gambler. Married several times. Has bouts of terrifying, uncontrollable rage. That sort of thing.'

'What was it like in the jungle?'

'Terribly uncivilised. Really rather sordid.'

'What did you eat?'

'Oh berries, I think. The odd bit of donated fish paste or rice.'

'What did you do all day?'

'Well, I used to kill Burmese soldiers by firing arrows made from coat hangers dipped in human excrement.'

I choke on my tea.

'You're joking.'

'No, not really.'

How he made the transition from aesthete to guerrilla fighter, or indeed back again, I have no idea. He is the least likely person you could possibly imagine tiptoeing through the jungle with a blow-dart contraption. He carefully stubs out his cigarette by bending the filter over the burning end, wipes down his crease-free Italian trousers, and stands up.

'Well, I must be off. Have a pleasant day.'

★　　★　　★

My last attempt at gaining contacts is with a well-known journalist who has been to Burma and met Aung San Suu Kyi. He suggests I don't go anywhere near her in case 'a brick is dropped on your head'.

And then my friends deliver the usual scaredy-cat soundbites.

'It's terribly dangerous, you really shouldn't go, the government will hold you at gunpoint, you'll be in a Burmese prison for months, they'll throw away the key.'

Suitably freaked by this, and not knowing how I'll react to Southeast Asia or how Southeast Asia will react to me, I book the first couple of nights' stay in Rangoon through a travel agent. I ask him the usual questions:

Will I die of food poisoning?

Is there huge political unrest?

Are people dying of starvation there?

Will I get chucked out of the country?

And his reply to all of them is a long 'Nooooooh!' except the last, to which he says, 'Not unless you're a writer.'

Even the guidebooks suggest lying on the visa-application form if you have anything vaguely writerish about you, so his remark is not that comforting. I keep shtoom.

I book a guide for the first day, dinner the first night and a car to drive me around for a few days. It is incredibly expensive, but the travel agent says he is making absolutely no profit at all and it's the extortionate price of petrol out there that is siphoning money out of my purse.

'I don't mind as long as none of this money is going to

the government,' I say. 'You're not associated with them, are you?'

I'm by now intensely paranoid.

'Nooooooooh!' comes the inevitable reply.

Waiting for my visa is a nail-biting experience as by now I am fascinated by the country, have totally set my heart on going and can't bear the idea of not being allowed to. Next day at the embassy I'm shaking like a leaf – and don't stop shaking until I'm in my hotel bedroom on the other side of the world.

PART TWO

BURMA

THREE

RANGOON

IN A DOTTY moment I have opted for a ridiculous money-saving scheme that takes me to Rangoon via Bangkok, Prague and Dubai.

The plane is from the seventies. The chairs, which are horribly narrow, flip forward into crash position all too easily and the safety video features a cross between Rasputin and Dracula. In my new Buddhist mode I am already missing my hairbrush (bird's-nest hair) and lip gloss (lips dry and tight) when an Austrian hippie boy behind with long straggly hair and rancid beer breath leans forward.

He wants to know how much I paid for my ticket.

'Too much, considering the conditions,' is my reply.

'Is it your first time in Bangkok?'

'Yes, it is.'

'Are you going to Khao San Road?'

'No, I'm going to Burma.'

'Maybe we could share a taxi?'

'To *Burma*?'

He breathes more beer breath over me.

'I'm a psychiatric nurse.'

'Are you? That's lovely.'

'*Ja*. Here is a photo of my woman.'

'Oh! Are you sure she'd want me to see this photo?'

'*Ja*, sure, why not?'

'Well, she's totally naked for a start.'

'*Ja*, it's OK.'

'Gosh, she's very supple, isn't she?'

'*Ja*, it's OK.'

From Bangkok, I fly to Rangoon. I am terrified that I won't get into the country. That I'll be frogmarched at gunpoint back on to a plane the second my feet hit the tarmac. But of course the airport is full of customs people quietly stamping passports and everyone getting on with their business. And what an airport. Very clapboard, very shed-like, very small and unimpressive. Everything brown and dusty and grimy and seventies. But I am in! The heat hits me like a slap in the face.

I'm picked up by a Chinese boy called Minmin, whose role is unclear, and by my driver for the next few days, whose name sounds like Gee Whizz. His teeth are totally black. Every now and then he opens the car window and spits long and throatily out of it. When we pass another car we honk, regardless of whether they are anywhere near us or not.

First I hit the seventy-year-old Bogyoke Aung San market. Just to see it, not to buy anything, you understand, as my limited understanding of Buddhism means the desire for material goods is a no-no. It's a dark hall packed with stalls selling jewellery, cloth, lacquerware, T-shirts, flip-flops (worn by absolutely everyone), cheroots, cigars, colourful shoulder bags with long tassels (typical of the Shan states) and cheap plasticware from China.

Everyone around me (men and women) is dressed in a lungi. This is a long cool skirt made from two pieces of material sewn together. The men wear theirs with the sides brought to the centre and twisted together. The women's have long ties at the side. Of course I haven't been in the place two minutes before I've bought two. I put one on – it immediately falls to the ground revealing my white thighs. The women at the stall gasp and titter politely as they form a discreet circle around me. They all have a yellow paste on their faces – *thanakha*, a traditional beauty cream which also acts as a sunblock, made from the *thanakha* tree. Some have squares on each cheek, some have a line on their nose, like tame pastel war paint.

Newly clad in my lungi I sit at a noodle stall outside the market, on a tiny plastic stool, perfect for a small three-year-old, less well equipped to deal with my bum. The sun is walloping down on my head. I can see I'm the cause of unbridled mirth for the locals. Whether it's my skin, my attempt at Burmese dress, or just general twitness emanating uncontrollably from me, I can't tell. Either way, they're shaking with laughter.

A fat woman seated behind mounds of noodles takes a generous handful, adds some raw vegetables and coconut soup, stirs the lot with her hands and passes it to me with a smile. I wash it down with delicious lime-and-sugar water.

A man sits next to me and talks quietly and brokenly about Burma not being democratic, and the government taking everything away from the people, how they are forced from their homes to live like refugees. We smile and nod at each other so as to look as though we are talking about a game of golf next Sunday.

Suddenly a boy opposite shouts, 'Manhesta Oonited!'

At this my companion scuttles off.

'Yes. Football,' I shout back, somewhat unnecessarily.

'Davee Bekkum! Po Spice!'

Christmas night. They're famous even over here.

It's very sunny, very hot and very humid. Before my big search for Burmese cats, I decide to pay homage to the big cats in the zoo. On the way I pass an enormous red sign with white letters. It says:

- Oppose those relying on external elements, acting as stooges, holding negative views.
- Oppose those trying to jeopardise stability of the state and progress of the nation.
- Oppose foreign nations interfering in internal affairs of the state.
- Crush all internal and external destructive elements as the common enemy.

Spooky.

According to the guidebook the zoo is a pleasant place to walk and relax and isn't too touristy. You're telling me.

I'm the only tourist here and everyone stares unashamedly. The women smile shyly and the men walk in front of me, their heads turned at 180 degrees to get a good look. I have to shout 'Look out!' a couple of times when they get close to trees. And no shift dress and stilettos for me. I am dressed, perhaps for the first time in my life, completely appropriately.

As is to be expected, the big cats in their grey concrete cages aren't even slightly excited about my search around Burma for the perfect Burmese cat. The lion is zonked out by the heat, and the tiger paces an interminable figure of eight.

From my stash of Biros and lipsticks, I give my first pen away to a little boy who looks at me as if to say, 'Another bloody Biro. All these tourists bring is pens. I want a Gameboy. Or at least some cash.'

I attempt conversation with the locals. The language is on a par with Japanese and Arabic for ease of comprehensibility. The writing is made up of a row of Christmas-ball decorations, some with wisps of hair from the top, others open at the sides. The posters have slogans such as 'Sure to win if you think win!', which presumably is the Burmese equivalent of Californian positive thinking.

This evening Minmin accompanies me to the Kayaweik for dinner, a concrete boat on the Kandawgi Lake, with multi-coloured lights in a Chinese pagoda style, all gold lacing on the roof and dragony bits. It's touristy with brightly silked girls dancing to loud crashing tinkly tinkly music in the classically stylised Burmese tradition, their thumb and third finger together, their wrists twisted out and curving round, as they hop about the stage like colourful birds. The music takes some getting used to. After a while it sounds less clashing discordance and more rhythm. Each dance relates a story – the princess is carried off by the ogre, who does not touch her because he can tell she doesn't love him – but the tourists, mainly Chinese, don't understand and don't clap. They're just heads down into the trough.

The food is excellent – rice with prawn curry, chicken curry, unidentifiable meat curry. The puddings are so pretty: tiny pieces of paw-paw, melon and mango followed by *copper mong*, a sort of jelly, half coconut and half jaggery, and *monlimia*, two little sugary dumplings one on top of the other, also known as husband and wife. Minmin offers me *lahpeq thouq* – moist green tea-leaves mixed on a teaspoon with fried garlic, peas, sesame seeds, dried prawn, ginger and peanuts and then popped in the mouth. Gently eye-watering. (Sadly, only tourists can afford such cuisine.)

Minmin's life is constricted. He stays at home watching videos all day because the university is closed down. When I ask him what he thinks of the government closing down the universities he replies, 'I not interested in politics,' and looks shifty. Instead he tells me that he never even spoke to a girl before he was seventeen and that he stills blushes puce when he does.

My guide is small, smiley and young – twenty-four but married with a child. He and his wife live at his parents' home with his brother and *his* wife. He tells me his name, but it is a jumble of phonetics and try as I might I cannot squeeze it into my head – Cheyawmi? Jaymeelah? He speaks very little English, which normally would be understandable, except I've paid a large sum of money for his services. Minmin is with us, but as the day progresses he is more melting wax figurine than man – sweat pours off him in rivulets. He is tall and soft – his white puppy fat bends his shoulders and belly forward creating a visible S in his back. His long arms dangle huge floppy white hands at their ends. His knees are big.

Gee Whizz drives us to several *payas* – Kava Aye, Botataung, Chaukhtatgyi and finally the Shwedagon. We take our shoes off before we enter. When the English colonised Burma there was an incredible fuss about the removing of shoes. In direct opposition to an 'In Rome do as . . .' gesture, the British absolutely refused to take their shoes off when entering *payas*, causing great offence. The Burmese had in the past gone to war over just this issue. In the thirteenth century King Narathihapaté had envoys from Kublai Khan executed for wearing their shoes too often – and Kublai Khan reciprocated by sacking Bagan a few years later. The British ambassadors in the nineteenth century thought having to take their shoes off was demeaning, and that, as representatives of a Great Empire, they should be exempt from showing respect to their hosts.

Outside the Kava Aye, the marble is ow-ow boiling, but in the covered areas it is cool, cool, smooth to the feet.

Donation boxes crammed with notes are dotted around. The money helps gild the Buddhas and maintain the *payas*. The Buddhas, with their elongated ear lobes (a sign of noble birth), are either white or gold. The Burmese prefer them to be gold. There is something hieroglyphic, simple, almost childish about the sculpture of the Buddhas. This is because art here is not for the promotion of the artist as in the West; the artist is merely a vessel for higher powers. Egotism is pointless as the artist's role is to reproduce the tried and tested formula as closely as possible. These Buddhas have been designed so that each element is in perfect balance with the rest. Sweet jasmine laces the air around the *paya*.

Next we visit the Botataung. My guide tells me no history about the place, so we smile encouragingly at each other.

'Here Buddha sacred hair,' says Minmin.

'Fabulous. Let's see how it's getting on after all this time.'

'No. Women not allowed into the inner sanctum.'

'Oh. Why not?'

'Women inferior, cannot attain nirvana.'

'Oh. Well, is it the inner sanctum that's the problem or the hairs themselves? How about his toe-nail clippings? Can I have a peek at those?'

But Minmin is walking through the corridors of the inner sanctum, which are covered floor to ceiling in a mosaic of blue, silver and gold mirrors – reflecting light in every direction. It is lovely. I wait outside, contenting myself with trying to identify a world religion that isn't inherently chauvinistic (I can't) and admiring the glass cases containing silver and gold Buddhas offered by wealthy people.

The *Bo* (meaning leader) *tataung* (meaning one thousand) refers to the thousand soldiers who brought back relics of the Buddha from India two thousand years ago. We stop in one covered area to admire a large bronze Buddha in a light airy hall. There are people sleeping on the floor, and further back groups of women chatting quietly, seated on their haunches, snacking on fruit. The serious worshippers near the front kneel and bow three times to the Buddha, their hands clasped together in prayer touching their foreheads as they rise and their hands flat out on the floor as they go down in supplication. They then make offerings of garlands of flowers or candles to the Buddha.

I am quite confused by the concept of offerings, as the Buddha is not a god, merely an enlightened human being. My guide explains that the offerings are in honour of the life the Buddha lived, and a means of helping us concentrate on the Buddhist scriptures. He also says that the Buddha is called Nanoo and that Nanoo went to England during Mindon's reign, but Queen Victoria got a headache and only when she sent Nanoo back to Burma did she feel better again. According to the guidebook this is all a load of guff, but I like the story anyway. I also love the fact that if you want to help gild the *paya*, you pay your money, and then the gilt is put into a little trolley by a serious lady with a shiny black topknot like Wilma from *The Flintstones*. The trolley is then winched above your head on a mini ski-lift system to the roof, where a guy sits all day waiting to apply the gilt to the roof.

Chaukhtatgyi has an enormous reclining Buddha whose feet are covered in lines and markings. Apparently when he was a child, one hundred soothsayers were asked to identify the Buddha from his feet and only one identified him correctly. The Buddha is housed in a shed-like structure with a corrugated-iron roof, and palm readers sit in the arms that spread out from the central courtyard. Astrology is an important part of Buddhist life – my guide sees an astrologer twice a month – and purely as a means of understanding this beautiful country, but in no way wishing to learn of future personal love and success, you understand, I plonk myself down at one of the astrologers and Minmin translates. The guy asks my birthday and after a protracted amount of calculation declares triumphantly that I am thirty-one. Actually I'm thirty, I whisper to Minmin, who whispers it back to him. The man looks doubtful and then assures me I am thirty-one. I don't want to argue, but this is something of an unwelcome surprise.

He then consults books, makes calculations in pencil on tiny pieces of paper and tells me I am:

angry (yup)
naughty and proud to my parents (nope)
greedy for money (yup)

due to marry within three months (Christmas night,
    that's terrifying)

due for a promotion (no job, so unlikely)

not great with Saturday-born men, but fine with
    Monday-born (fair enough)

and about to have stomach problems (not unpre-
    dictable).

He then asks me what I do. Because my guidebook
assures me there are government agents sniffing around
everywhere, ready to pounce on any Burmans hanging
out with foreigners, especially foreign writers, I don't want
to endanger Minmin and my guide, so I'm flexible with
the truth. Not that it makes much difference. He merely
tells me I should release some birds, give a donation to the
Buddha, pour water on the Wednesday shrine thirty-one
times, give flowers and light a candle.

His predictions have been predictable, until Minmin
shouts out, 'And a goat!'

'A what?'

'A goat!'

'A goat? A *goat*? What about a goat?'

'Yes! Yes! He says you have a goat! You love him,
though. He not frightened!'

'Why would I have an unfrightened goat?'

Flummoxed, but outwardly serene, I let Minmin and
Guide decide that I should give my donation at the most
impressive of all *payas* – the Shwedagon. On our way back
to the taxi, we are surrounded by women carrying cages of

birds. Buddhists believe it is extremely good for the soul to release other souls – and I can't bear the sight of the birds all cramped and miserable in there. Soon I am surrounded by women and boys holding out nervy twitterers in their hands, so I buy as many as I can afford, and there is a satisfying moment each time I feel the feathery heartbeat and then for less than a fraction of a second the scratchy flutter as I open my hand and the bird is off. The sellers clearly think their Christmases and Tuesdays have all come at once. They are laughing and joking amongst themselves as they take turns to give this silly sentimental Western girl her kick. The bird is gone in a whirr, its wings beating like a hummingbird, whizzing low up into the nearest tree and then further up and away. Minmin leans over and whispers that the sellers merely catch the birds again later, that some of them have been released several times, which makes me feel slightly hopeless.

My relationship with Minmin is coming under strain. Whenever I want to buy something he shouts 'Bargain! Bargain! Offer at least half!' I know he is trying to help me, but everything is so cheap, I can't bear to wrestle for a few kyat from people who clearly have so little anyway. He loses his temper when I don't understand his English, which is somewhat unfair considering it is closer to Swahili than anything else. Having said that I am completely grateful to him and realise how ridiculous it is to wander into this country without having learnt the language first.

He and the guide treat me like a princess – it's car door

open and best table in restaurants all day. I respond with a constant inane smile on my face – and realise that this false security is what I paid my money for. Everything is easy – too easy. I do feel safe, but I also feel mollycoddled, protected from anything real, and therefore slightly numb. I also feel as though the only people my money is helping is the travel agent, who isn't even Burmese anyway, Minmin reminds me – he's Chinese. To have any type of business means he must in some way be cooperating with the government. Already I feel implicated.

The Shwedagon is the most sacred of the Buddhist sites. It burns gold in the heat of the sun and radiates reddish glory as the sun sets. Its towering *stupa* is set with an enormous 76-carat diamond at the very top of its vane, and just below that are more than 5,000 smaller diamonds. There is gold everywhere, not least because below the magnificent *stupa* are many smaller *stupas*, shrines, temples and *zedis* – as though it has mushroomed children at its feet.

Guide tells me that the Shwedagon is 2,500 years old – which is true in that there has been a *zedi* here for that amount of time, but due to earthquakes the Shwedagon has been rebuilt many times – most recently in the eighteenth century. I rely on my guidebook for the rest of the story behind the Shwedagon: apparently two merchant brothers met the Buddha and were given eight of his hairs to bring back to Burma. They built a shrine because previous Buddha relics were buried here. And when the hairs were transferred from their casket, everything went a bit haywire, gems falling to earth, trees blossoming out of season, lightning, hurricanes, earthquakes, that sort of thing.

Walking up the cool pathways I am not tempted by the plethora of items for sale – ivory combs, paper flowers, books, incense – because in my conversion to Buddhism I have no desire for these material things. We follow the crowd, walking clockwise, until we reach the Wednesday shrine. I am slightly confused by the fact that the Burmese count an eight-day week – Wednesday being split into morning Wednesday and evening Wednesday, represented by a little elephant statue either with or without tusks. I dutifully pour water over one of the elephants thirty-one times from a little cup and fountain right next to it. I light my candle, offer some jasmine as novice nuns in pink robes and with shaven heads scuttle by. They walk apart from the novice boy monks, who are in dark-red robes.

Guide and I sit underneath one of the many shrines. We chat pidgin. The bobbing halts and stutters of our sentences make the process exhausting for both of us. For no apparent reason, he says that according to the *thekkayit* calendar it is 1363, but the Burmese also use the Gregorian calendar, and the Buddhist Era calendar, which says it is 2543. Very confusing. But he's such a nice guy. We smile constantly at each other.

Afterwards we wander through the Chinese market with Minmin – it's full of pink-and-green plastic guns, plastic combs, cheap alarm clocks, sunglasses, dresses, dried prawns in a great pinkish mound with flies swarming around, sesame seeds, spiky jack fruit, mangoes and watermelon.

Small wizened men squat over camping stoves and cook little fried dumplings with eggs on top, or grill sticks of pork, chicken and squid on open barbecues. Looking up, I see washing hanging from balconies and great swathes of plaster peeling off the walls and dirty cardboard faded posters.

Having booked Gee Whizz for a few days, all I have to do now is decide where we are to go tomorrow. The guidebook ominously says nothing about Burmese cats, so I go straight to reception, to lovely Daw Chee.

Silly Conversation Number 1:

'Oh hello, I wonder if you could help me?'

I sound so English, reserved and ridiculous.

She looks bewildered for a second.

'Yes?'

'Do you know where I can find Burmese cats?'

She looks really bewildered for a second.

'Chats?'

'Cats!'

'*Nats*? Buhmez *nats*?'

'Mmm, yes,' wondering if we're talking about the same thing, but realise I have to make allowances for accents – hers, all swallows and vowels, and mine, all glottal stops and St Trinian's clips.

We look at each other wildly for a second – our minds whirring, but no cogs actually clicking in.

'You laak visit *nats*?'

'Yes! Burmese ones. Brown? Meow?'

I put two hands up behind my head and pull my hands

out in a long moustache gesture to indicate whiskers. She looks completely dumbstruck.

'Bagan!' finally she says with a smile.

'Bagan?'

'Yes, full of *nats*! Very good place for *nats* – many-years-old nats!'

'Oh excellent, well, thank you so much.'

I am very pleased I now have a place to direct Gee Whizz to. I'm looking forward to a long drive with him. Even though we don't speak a word of each other's language, his face and eyes show a nice soul, and body language and gestures will get us through, I feel. He doesn't look that thrilled when I tell him, and Minmin tells me it is at least a fourteen-hour drive. Better than a bus, I say, and at least Gee Whizz will be earning well this month. Gee Whizz smiles, his teeth as black as ever. Black, I now realise, from the betel he constantly chews. Betel-wrapped areca-nut is a mild stimulant which provokes constant spitting – slightly stomach-churning – but Gee Whizz is very discreet and we always smile at each other after he has successfully disgorged some saliva without too much noise. I won't tell him that I used to deworm Claudius using an areca-nut extract.

FOUR

PYAY TO BAGAN

TODAY A SIX-hour drive to Pyay – which is halfway to Bagan. Gee Whizz turns up early, but is not alone. Mr Chow, Minmin's father and the owner of the travel agency, has decided I am important enough to accompany us to Bagan, which is annoying. I'm much happier on my own. But perhaps he is there to help Gee Whizz with the driving. After a few hours I realise it is not that. Nor is it to chat to him and keep him awake during the long hours ahead, because he doesn't say a word. I think it is just to protect me, but as foreigners are safer here than the natives, I can't think why.

The first thing we do is bless the car. This involves stopping at a special car shrine, where Gee Whizz reverses and advances the car three times, in a mechanical bow to Buddha. A boy drops jasmine over our rear mirror and sings incantations while spraying the car with holy water.

'Sae chuhknee,' smiles Mr Chow.

('Safe journey' – I think.)

The roads are extraordinary, not least because of the dogs lying asleep in them. Which is proof enough, I think, for anyone not yet convinced, that dogs are a hell of a lot more stupid than cats. Dogs may be whacked by hand or booted by foot, but cars pose no problem for them – probably because Buddhists are so anti-killing they drive around the dog instead of honking it out of the road as it surely deserves. The roads are single-lane, bumpy, pot-holed affairs, where every car honks at every car (three for a bus) even when it is not overtaking. Meanwhile the heat grabs you by the ears and looks you in the eye and promises not to let up for a second. It is ten in the morning. The roads are occupied by bicycles, trishaws, honking buses, lorries laden with logs, girls under umbrellas (not bamboo parasols) and cycles balancing under many layers of corrugated-iron sheets.

As we move out of Rangoon, the brick houses become woven matted huts with thatched bamboo-leaf roofs on wooden stilts. We pass endless rice paddies, many with gilded mini shrines in the middle and water with lilac lotuses floating on top, pink bougainvillaea and jacaranda. Mr Chow hands over money at the many checkpoints we pass. In each town there is also a stall with loud jingly-jangly tinny music and lines of girls shaking bowls for donations to the local pagoda. We don't slow down but Mr Chow regally holds out his hand, drops the money, we whizz past, the note whirls up into the air like a leaf and the girl chases after us to catch it as though chasing a butterfly.

This is how we spend two days: driving for hours in silence, eating Chinese food in silence behind a curtain away from the locals (because Mr Chow will not allow me to eat Burmese food). He utters the odd 'Chorlet?'

every few hours. (I am drinking eight litres of water a day due to the immense heat.) I can see him thinking: Why didn't the silly cow take the plane like all the other tourists? Or at least the bus if she wants the full experience? But my intention was to give money to local drivers who needed it. I realise that Mr Chow, who is far from poor, is taking most of this, so when he's not looking I give Gee Whizz a hefty tip, which he pockets speedily, without a hint of surprise or gratitude. Giving is an inherent part of Buddhism, and does me good, therefore his taking the money is a favour to me. So I also give him one of my lungis for his wife, as I reckon a really good Buddhist wouldn't have bought it in the first place.

The day's highlight as we approach Pyay is Shwedaung, where a huge image of a Buddha sits with large gold glasses perched on the end of his nose like a newsreader. People come here from miles around, as the Buddha is believed to cure ailments, especially connected to the eyes. The glasses are removed by nine monks every two weeks for a cleaning.

When settled in our foul, dirty hotel, I nip off for a quick tour of Pyay. Quickly Mr Chow and Gee Whizz are at my side like lackeys. I sign-language that I'm happy alone, but Gee Whizz genuinely doesn't understand, and Mr Chow does, but doesn't want me to go out on my own. On a microcosmic scale, I feel as the people in this country must: my intentions are innocent, but I'm not allowed to do what I want. It's oppressive and frustrating. I wander around town, Mr Chow shadowing me like a guilty secret. Everyone is very smiley and friendly. They shake hands with me and smile and then run giggling back to their friends. I can't really talk to anyone because the moment I do Mr Chow is by my side, making me feel like I'm in a Hitchcock film. I'm not sure they've ever seen a white girl by herself before.

'You only one?' everyone asks, astonished.

'Yup, it's just me,' I reply, trying to look proud and independent. But they manage to make me feel I'm in the wrong even more than my married friends in Notting Hill. The truth is the Burmese girls rarely go out by themselves, let alone travel. So they think I'm a bit strange. Worst thing is, it's catching. *I'm* beginning to think I'm a bit strange.

I make my way to a trishaw. But Mr Chow is by my side instantly. He tells the trishaw to go to the hotel. I gesture a tour around town first. Mr Chow nods and then tells the driver to go straight to the hotel, because that's what he wants to do. But back at the hotel, I gesture to the driver to carry on. Bemused for a moment he then starts humming to himself and cycles slowly off.

The sun is low in the sky – an unutterably lovely time of day. We arrive at a park by the river where young boys and girls sway on rusty swings. I walk down the jetty to the wide, calm and golden-brown Irrawaddy. The sun on the other side of the water burns orange and big. Half the town is washing, paddling about and enjoying the almost bearable late-day heat. The girls swim covered in their lungis and the boys are naked apart from their lungis tied up through their legs like shorts. As boys run past me to the water, they shout 'Hello!'. Others run past and shout 'Goodbye!' with the same intonation as 'Hello!'. One man proudly points at his partner and smiles 'My why!'. It's all rather charming.

I want to swim too but don't think it appropriate. And then I think what the hell. I must wash off the dirt in my bones after hours in the car. I tiptoe, fully clothed, into the river. There is a full silence as the locals stop what they are doing and watch. Suddenly I feel very foolish. But then the boys whoop and yell their approval and the girls giggle and whisper to each other behind their hands. Smiling widely, looking actually not unlike a white crocodile, I breast-stroke past everyone out into the river. Impromptu races break out amongst the boys who front-crawl past me, their heads swinging from side to side, throwing out drops of water like suburban garden sprinklers, as their arms flail over their hair. I tread water out there, my clothes billowing around me like watery parachutes.

Looking back to shore, I see Mr Chow standing on the edge waving frantically at me. What's wrong? Has my bag been stolen from the hotel? Has Gee Whizz dropped down dead? I swim back quickly, worried. Closer to the shore, I see his face is wrinkled in anger. Climbing out of the water, my clothes like lead weights, I feel suddenly self-conscious, that the shape and imprints of my body are evident through my thin clothes. Mr Chow doesn't say a word, but turns on his heel imperiously. I follow him sheepishly up to the car where Gee Whizz is waiting.

I don't know whether he's angry because I gave him the

slip, or because I've contravened some Burmese code and swum in the river, but he doesn't seem in the mood to explain. Gee Whizz looks apologetic but also as though he's about to giggle – which is catching. We suddenly burst into hysterical fits of laughter. Mr Chow mumbles something in Burmese but our laughter rocks the car to the extent that he heaves a sigh, gives up and waves Gee Whizz on like a tired royal. We go straight to dinner. Luckily the heat soon deals with my dripping clothes, as Gee Whizz and I share cigarettes and let slip the odd chuckle. Mr Chow orders my dinner as usual.

'Local!' he says menacingly.

'Delicious,' I smile defiantly. 'That's why I'm here – to try the local food.'

We sit ourselves down on plastic chairs under neon lights; there are cheap plastic pictures on the wall. I nibble at slices of green mango (hard and bitter) in a hot sauce. There is a spicy bouillon-type soup to go on the rice. The main course arrives. It is completely unrecognisable. In short it is the aquatic version of *Apocalypse Now*, so blackened and charred with all its bones showing that it is more cartoon than food. I look horrified, Mr Chow looks triumphant and Gee Whizz almost has a heart attack from laughing. He starts coughing the way cats do when they have hair balls in their throat: his head protruding from his neck, moving back and forth in short sharp bursts like a turtle. The entire world stops and waits until he's finished. The waiter cuts it up for me, head bones and all, and that's how it is meant to be eaten. I chew it, and make lots of

'Mmm, my *favourite*' noises, determined to enjoy it. It tastes very strange.

Next morning, back in the car, with hours ahead of us until Bagan. But at least there will be cats. Our days are of dust and dirt. Mr Chow is in a slightly better mood because I've taught him a new word – 'good'. We try it out a few times.

Silly Conversation Number 2:

'I didn't sleep last night.'

'Good good.'

'Not one wink.'

'Good good.'

'My last boyfriend didn't love me.'

'Good.'

'Nor I him, actually.'

'Yus, fie fie.'

My stomach and head are in revolt at last night's fish. We make more pit stops than before and Mr Chow makes chortly 'heh heh heh' noises every time I rush, my hands clutching my stomach, to one loo after the other.

At one restaurant, the owner hurries up to me.

'For ever your face will be stamped on my memory. I will never forget you. You are always welcome. I learn English in missionary school. You very important guest.'

Oh! He speaks English. What luck.

'Your restaurant is absolutely lovely. Do you have any cats?'

He looks blank.

'Solly?'

'Your restaurant. I like it.'

I chicken out.

He looks worried and then says, 'Oh!' with his finger Confucius-style in the air. He takes a deep breath.

'For ever your face will be stamped on my memory. I will never forget you. You are always welcome. I learn English in missionary school. You very important guest.'

As we drive on to Bagan, we pass women walking along the roads with heavy pails of water hanging from long sticks strung across their shoulders, and people working in the roads, women, children, men, breaking up large stones into smaller ones. I've read articles about forced labour and I'm pretty sure this is it. The heat is horrifically strong, and as we drive past Mr Chow hands them bottles of water. Their eyes are large and anxious – and they flicker disappointment when they see water and not money. The bottles have stickers that say: 'Warranty: on water absence of e coli and pathogenic organisms'. Most comforting. Lorries pass us with twenty people inside and twenty people on top.

The endless driving, as well as the fish from last night, has me feeling fizzy, fuzzy, wobbly. The land around us is horribly dry and dusty. The mass clearing of trees for cultivating fields has caused Burma immense eco problems. The UN is helping to plant more trees – as all the teak trees have been sold to the Thais, who have built permanent roads into the jungles to ensure they can fell logs all year round; but whenever I ask Mr Chow if we can stop to read the signs outlining the UN projects, he mumbles at Gee Whizz to drive on.

I feel so lonely with Mr Chow. Everyone we see is smiley and friendly, but he creates a barrier that is impossible to breach.

We drive all day. Finally we arrive in Bagan. There is an entry fee to the town which I know goes straight to the government, and induces a twinge of guilt. Mr Chow and Gee Whizz drive me to my hotel, which is in the old archaeological zone. As we drive further in, temples and pagodas dot the plains for miles around, like ancient chess pieces mid-game, as far as the eye can see. It is an awesome sight. The sun is again low in the sky. Gee Whizz and I smile and shake hands warmly. But Mr Chow and I are happy to see the back of each other.

'I'd just like to say, Mr Chow' – I hold on to his hand and shake it really vigorously up and down like a pump – 'that it's thanks to people like you that this government is still running. If your countrymen had a little knowledge of human rights, they'd refuse to trade with Burma. I wanted my money to go to the Burmese, not the Chinese.'

He of course does not understand a word of this, but I feel better nevertheless.

The hotel is very luxurious. It's a clean-proper-air-conditioning-manicured-gardens-uniformed-servants-lifting-covers-off-food kinda place. There is a terrace overlooking the river with swish types sipping cocktails. Yippee. I am so happy to be free of Mr Chow at last that I invent a sort of tribal dance, oochee oochee, humbugga

humbugga, a mix between the back scissor chop and policemen's hokey kokey bend. Unfortunately I didn't close my bedroom door before starting this.

'Massah?'

The porter is standing at the door.

'Massage? You bet, baby.'

'Five dollar hour?'

'You betcha. Tonight at eight.'

While freshening up I decide that the main bane of being a Buddhist is its effect on my hair. Without my brush, my hair is a matted mess. Without my tweezers I am Denis Healey. And without my razor I wake with my arms stretched up and think a tarantula is lying under my arm. Disgusting.

At the next-door hotel for dinner. The food is good, but very expensive, and I am the only tourist there. But I love being dignified, no drinking, no swearing, sitting up properly, no betraying any emotions. Fabulous. If only I'd known that behaving well was this much fun.

A beautiful bird practising its scales up and down the warble, then 'do doo, do doo' like a doorbell keeps me company throughout dinner, as well as the waiter who every few minutes comes over and gives my bowl of rice a three-quarters turn just in case I have forgotten it. The waiter says the bird is an 'oohdwal' which I think is his way of saying 'owl' because when I ask how you spell it he says 'Oo weebelwee low'. Then another waiter contradicts him and says it is a kikko – a very sticky lizard with a red mouth, poisonous and ugly to boot. I have no idea who is right or what is what. So no change there then.

The thing with travelling on your own is that everything takes half the normal time. So dinner is done and dusted in thirty minutes. Back at the hotel I have just the TV for company as the sun has now set over the calm Irrawaddy, and the blue dusk has hollowed out to a heavy dark. MTV Asia has an interview with Christina Aguilera who is the most intense airhead. A total no-brain. Though in Spanish it means 'eyrie', in English Aguilera sounds less appetising, more like a particularly nasty water-borne disease. But on the other side is the Burmese news. A small, unhappy reader with a bowl-cut reads the news, which is interspersed with clips from CNN in unsubtitled English. But enough of this massaged truth, this false news of booming economy and smiling generals and opened schools and happy people. It is time for my own massage.

Clammy hands, fast movements, the man breathes heavily and is completely unrelaxed. It occurs to me that he is not an official hotel masseur. My upset stomach means I can't relax either in case I trumpet my sick state to him. After a while he turns me on to my back and I signal that my top is to stay on. He puts his hand on it.

'No,' I say.

'Yes,' he says.

'No.'

'Yes.'

He takes it off. I'm paralysed and unable to stop him.

'Get yer filthy hands orf me,' is what I want to say but I am unable to.

Through facial grimaces and gestures he insists it is not a proper massage otherwise. After a few minutes, when he didn't really touch my chest but had a good gawp instead, he gives my top back. I feel foolish, taken advantage of and annoyed that I didn't stand up for myself.

There's no point in wanting independence unless you act it out. No matter. Apparently that ultimate symbol of independence, the cat, is to be found here in Bagan. So what if today I am hopelessly isolated and needlessly groped. Tomorrow is a new day and there are cats out there waiting to be discovered.

Walking this morning in the direction of the temples, I am stopped by a guy with yellow eyes like a cat and – like a spider – soft black spiky hair, which has grown straight out from a formerly shaved head. It seems reluctant to relax down near his ears. Maung, who speaks excellent English, wants $8 a day for being my guide. It's hefty by local rates, but as far as I'm concerned he's worth his weight in gold. We make our way to the temples in the back of a cloppety horse and carriage. We move slowly, slowly, past temples and shrines and *stupas* in Bagan's strange light, that twenties-film, sepia-tinted, dappled light of morning.

At Thilomilo temple, Maung tells me the story of the king's umbrella. 'The king eldy son don wan be heir, so king stood his five ons round open umbrella. He twir it, it point to one who be king. So they say king one umbrella, one umbrella king.'

In one temple there is a circular wishing shrine, where a choice of money-bowls is signposted in English: 'May you win lottery', 'May you pass examination', 'May you meet those who loves you'. Buddhists clearly don't mind passing on to Buddha the usual shopping list of worldly requirements.

Bagan reached its peak with King Anawrahta's succession in 1044. He was converted to Theravada Buddhism by a monk sent specially for that purpose by Manuha, the Mon King of Thaton. King Anawrahta then asked for several important religious scripts to be sent to him, and when Manuha refused, Anawrahta marched his army to Thaton, captured the city, the city's monks and scholars, the King, his white elephants and every religious text he could get his hands on. They were brought to Bagan, and Anawrahta then started an immense period of building. There are 2,217 monuments in the area built by the King and his successors over a period of 250 years. Now many are tumbling down but in its heyday, the place was a blaze of gold-and-silver-bejewelled turrets and spires. Bagan came to the end of its glory years with an invasion by Kublai Khan and his Mongols. It was then inhabited by looters and robbers from the fourteenth to eighteenth century, but people started settling here again once the colonists provided some protection from the looters.

Learning about the temples, and gilding various Buddhas,

is pleasurable enough but listening to Maung talk about himself is even better.

'Yeah, cos I live in Harrow for a why buh thuh drink ee got to me, donit? I was in a bah way. I'ze livin' with these geezers and they had to pick me up off the floor now again. I here to clean up. My family here too in a house, isn't it?'

'In New Bagan?'

'Yeah, they moved us there from here.'

He sweeps his arm around him. He's referring to the enforced resettlement in 1990 just before the May elections. Families who had been in Old Bagan for many years were forced to resettle in a peanut field a few kilometres away from the temples. They were given a week to move. All trace of the livelihoods and villages in Old Bagan was removed.

'It was alive bevoh, you know, close to the gods. Now those hotels government-owned.'

'Hmm. *What?*'

'Your hotel is owned by the government.'

'But the guidebook says it's private.'

'Yeah, ees not. Anyone who owns somewhere like that is hand in hand with the government.'

'Then I must move. Do you know somewhere else?'

'Yeah. My friend owns a place. We can go there.'

A wave of guilt at the $21 already gone to the government momentarily mingles with regret that I'm leaving luxury – or Burmese-style luxury anyway, which is still pretty thin-walled and plastic-floored.

'So do you agree with Aung San Suu Kyi, and her views on tourists?'

'Yeah.'

This doesn't help my guilt.

'Big groups worse. You OK independent.'

Phew.

'Yes. I want my money to go direct to the people, OK? No big tourist places.'

'OK,' at which point he takes me to a restaurant for lunch, which is packed with tourists and very expensive.

'Maung?'

'Yeah?'

'This place?'

'Yeah? Oh solly. Is a bit pricey, yeah?'

'Yeah. Why're we here?'

'My brother owns it.'

Later we go to the market. Burmese women believe that squatting on their haunches is good for varicose veins and they sit by their baskets like that, looking very much as if they're going to the loo. They sell green tomatoes, tiny garlics, small red chillies, or huge bunches of red-and-pink daisies with yellow hearts. Maung takes me to a medicine man who sells me green licking powder. I pour it on my mit – it stinks of sulphur, disgusting it is too, but it calms my riotous stomach, which has been having a conversation of its own for days now. I give some children money and pretty soon an ugly smash-and-grab situation ensues. I give more and more, but they're insatiable.

★　　★　　★

My new room is dingy, with no natural light, and smells damp. Only thin red cotton strips of material hang from the windows. When we walk in, Maung's friends are asleep on the verandah floor with their grandchildren, whose sex it is difficult to distinguish. They shuffle up and blink and smile and look slightly disapprovingly at Maung.

'They worry I drinking still.'

'And are you?'

'Yeah. Def-nittly.'

We sit on the porch watching horses and carts clip and bicycles slip by.

'What wanna do, Tracey?'

'Tracey? Who's Tracey?'

'Oh solly. I think you other girl I spen tie with. Wass your name?'

'Clare.'

'Care. Yeah, thas right.'

'I'd like to see some cats.'

'Yeah? Really? OK.'

He takes some jasmine from the vase on the verandah table.

'Won't your friend miss that?'

'Nah, nah, ess OK.'

We borrow bicycles from his friend and cycle back towards Old Bagan. The heat is monstrous, ridiculous, a travesty. I am dripping wet within seconds and wondering if I can go on. Just before entering Old Bagan, we stop at the Tharaba Gateway, the only remains of the old ninth-century city wall. Maung gets off his bike, and puts some jasmine on the left-hand side of the gate and some on the right.

'Brother and sister *nats*, man Lord Handsome, woman Lady Golden Face. Died in a fire so we give them flowers, not candles or incense. Geddit?'

He looks very pleased with himself.

'That's very interesting, Maung. Thanks so much for showing me these, but where are the cats?'

'They here. They guard the city. The *nats*.'

'No – cats, I said.'

'*Oh!* Cats! Meow?'

He puts his hands up in the bunny position behind the head.

'Meow, yeah?'

'Yeah, meow.'

I'm getting the hang of Harrow Burmese lingo.

'Right! I thought you meant *nats* – the spiritual guardians we worship here.'

Suddenly I realise that perhaps my attention should go to the *nats* a bit more. They might help me find the cats.

'Do the Burmese have cats?'

'Oh yeah. Yeah. We like cats. They're not like dogs living on the scraps of humans, yeah? They're loved and kept at home.'

Which is a relief.

'Phew, it's hot. Shall we go swimming?' he says.

'Yup. Definitely.'

We cycle off to the Irrawaddy. Clambering down to the banks, we are the only ones there. So in need of cool am I that I don't bother with the guidebook in case it says: 'Instant pulverisation and disintegration if skin contacts river water.' The river is brown and green, peaceful, still, quiet, no banks but yellow mountains in the distance, no tourists, no one at all in fact, just one boatman punting a long canoe on the other side. Maung doesn't swim, he looks respectfully in the other direction even though I'm fully clothed. We're in the blinding heat of an afternoon sun, but the water is cool and fresh. It is wonderfully peaceful. Still I keep an eye out for floaters. And pray I don't catch Christina Aguilera.

'So, Maung, where are the *nats* and how can I learn about them?'

'OK. For tha you nee my mate Dow Tip. We mee him tomorrow.'

Right. Direction at last.

FIVE

BAGAN TO MANDALAY

BUT BEFORE TOMORROW comes, the sunset. The best place for sunsets in Bagan is on top of any of the thousands of temples strewing the plains. The Mingalazedi temple is particularly impressive. So I hit it. So do several other tourists. An official guide tells a rich German couple that the reason people had been moved from Old Bagan was because the river used to flood the village during the rainy season – the government version of events, I guess. I stay up there a while looking unconvincing, reading my book, with a 'Don't worry – you don't need to talk to me. I *love* being alone' look on my silly face. The truth is a chat (and a cat) would be nice. I would love to have dinner with some travellers, but everyone else up here is part of a couple and seems uninterested in talking. I too once enjoyed a sunset as part of a twosome, I want to tell them, but I have *chosen* to be alone.

I was eighteen and with a heavily proboscised Italian called Gianfranco. We were sitting on the walls of Radda, a medieval village in the middle of Chiantishire in Italy, drinking a bottle of Asti spumante – which tastes pretty much as it sounds, spew-worthy – because it was the last night of the *festa*. I had arrived in Italy with my boyfriend, George, but because of his recent confession that he had slept with someone else (and not the first infidelity either) I had cut my losses and was hanging out with someone more interesting and interested, watching the sunset. (The first time George was unfaithful, he told me about it as he poured a pot of tea for myself and the girl with whom he had done the deed, although I didn't realise it was her until that dreadful moment.

'I thought you'd laugh,' he said stupidly.

I cried.

'Oh don't worry, he loves you,' she smirked.

'But is this how he loves?' I sobbed back.)

Just a few hours before the Asti spumante, George and I had been in a tent in the garden of his mother's best friend's large whitewashed villa, whose portal was covered in blood-red roses and lilac wisteria. He was in a bate for some reason. I reached my hand over to him.

'Is this what you want?' he growled, forcing me, his muscled back curved over me like a powerful monkey.

I struggled and turned my head to the right, preferring to watch the woodlice scuttling over our musty-smelling blankets. After that he told me of his latest infidelity.

But I tried not to think about this as I sat with Gianfranco on the town walls, enjoying the *festa* and the sunset. Unfortunately, as Gianfranco cracked open a second bottle, George walked by. He double-took when he saw us.

'Gianfranco.' He smiled. 'If you touch her, I'll kill you.'

He walked off. He walked back.

'Clare, a word, please.'

I followed him. About ten metres away he burst into hysterical sobs.

'How can you do this to me?' he howled, as children with ice-cream-smeared mouths stared up at us, their lollies dripping to the floor, wondering how this scarlet woman could have done such a thing.

He smashed his hand against the wall until two drops of blood stood on his knuckles like ladybirds.

These strange memories crowd my thoughts, kiboshing my attempts to seem friendly. Is it right to love strongly, unreservedly, trustingly? Or should it be a dance of subtle revelation? Or should it be go with the flow? Oh I don't know. I wander back to my flea-pit hotel somewhat pensive in spite of, perhaps because of, the beautiful sunset which is still very high in the sky, behind the mist, like a bindi on an Indian woman's graceful head with a lilac-blue veil trailing behind.

And back in my dingy room I can't help crying about my various un-princed frogs. My tears drench several hankies, turning them into miniature soggy snowballs, which I line up along the edge of my bed like an emotional firing range of love mishaps to be blown out of my system once and for all.

Just then, Maung drops by and invites me to join him for supper. I am thrilled. He orders two large whiskies and grips them in his small curved monkey-like hands. Like most alcoholics, the moment he takes a sip, it opens some vast ancient reservoir in him so that he absolutely reeks of weeks' and months' worth of old alcohol in his veins. I don't drink with him because it's too hot still. His watery eyes wander around the restaurant.

'In London, I work in big hotel cleaning. I living in thirty-quid-week room with three others, but I had a brekdow, isn't it? But I OK – yeah, I used to diving and ducking. But I love drink. Yeah, I had good tie New Year's Eve lass yee. I told this guy I'ze tourist guide in Burma and he say really? How tall are the others and how many there? Ha! He thought I say taurus guy!'

I think he means tallest guy.

Maung's pronunciation means I often have to decipher things pretty speedily during the course of the conversation.

'I talking in the pool today . . .'

Is there a swimming place around here? Was he playing pool?

'But there were no suns . . .'

No sense? No signs? No suns?

'No dow . . .'

'No town? No way down? No, *dow* as in the polite form of addressing a lady over here?

'How old you?'

'Guess,' I say and immediately regret it.

The age-guessing game is a) self-indulgent, b) boring, c) forces the guesser into a false flattery situation, d) indicates extreme vanity on the part of the guessee. But luckily

Maung is too far gone to realise any of this and puts me firmly into mid-thirties.

'I'm thirty.'

'Oh yeah. You look younger than that.'

'Really?' I'm pleased but confused. 'But I have these lines,' pointing to my eyes.

To which he says, 'Yeah! You should plastic sujjily?'

'Why aren't you married, Maung?'

'I too old. I thirty-three. Gulls hee marry in early, early twenties. They not interested in me. Anyway I marry drink. *Ha!* Shall we eat chickool?'

When it arrives the meat is soft and spongy. The chicken is 90 per cent gristle, 5 per cent bone and 5 per cent skin. Frankly it is disgusting. We are quiet for a while, breathing and relaxing from the forced effort of understanding each other. We sink further down into our reveries as we crunch through our dinner.

After a while, apropos of nothing, Maung says, 'I fancy myself a little bit. I a bit arrogant.'

'Yeah. Me too,' I sigh.

At the end of the evening as I walk down the unlit street to my hotel, he shouts out, 'Night, Tracey!'

Back in my room, for a split second I think the management have left a sweet on my pillow, but looking closer realise it is the plasticy shiny curled-up body of a dead cockroach.

When sober, Maung finds Dow Tip, a driver, who takes me to Mount Popa where the thirty-seven major *nats* live. *Nats* are spirits that guard both the home and other areas, such as trees or forests or mountains. *Nat* worship predates Buddhism and now exists alongside it. *Nats* have their own festivals, known as *pwes*, often during the full or new moon. People appease them with offerings and ask for their protection. Mount Popa is an extinct volcano, where it is forbidden to eat pork, swear, say bad things about other people, or wear red or black. This might piss the *nats* off who could retaliate with a spate of bad luck.

Dow Tip wears aviator specs propped on his shaven head. He's just back from his annual seven-day stint as a monk. Believing that the monks eat very little, I wonder why he's rather porky, but later find out when I eat at a monastery that the monks eat better than anyone else in Burma. Buddhism is so engrained that even the poorest people give their best food to the monks and their last pennies to the temples. This culture of giving regardless of circumstances is impressive and inspirational.

The road to Mount Popa is one long dusty single-lane road. We're the only car on it. We stop on the way at a jaggery hut. The peasants shimmy up these horribly tall trees to cut down the cane. An old woman, smoking an enormous cheroot bigger than a carrot, then boils the cane in a wok. When it has melted it is heated further until it turns into a paste. This is then rolled into little balls and sold in bags as sweets. It is delicious, so sweet as to make the eyes bloodshot, but delicious. They also make alcohol from the fermented sugar.

We drive up the mountain. At the top there is still the

monastery to climb. As an offering for the *nats* I buy a jar of yellow champa flowers, which have been put in a special liquid to keep the colour, and start the ascent. (A bunch of flowers is fine but if you sniff them they are no longer a valid offering.)

A girl approaches me.

'My name Cho,' she smiles, and her friends burst out giggling.

I smile back at them.

Everyone notices me, looks at me, and many ask, 'Hello, where do you go?'

Some of them smile and seem happy with 'To the top!' even though it is not exactly illuminating. Others just want to practise their English and make their friends laugh, so they don't wait for an answer.

On the way up, there are no cats, but there are plenty of monkeys that are fat, fat, fat with nasty pink bottoms. This is because the tourists feed them grapes and other things they buy from stalls dotted on the steps on the way up. The monkeys' tiny hands fit snugly around the grapes. Some have babies, the size of fat rats, clinging to them. When they see what I have, they cling on to my skirt, and the physical contact is gratifying – shaking Mr Chow's hand and the massage were the last time I had human contact.

Less gratifying is the good hard pinch one little bugger gives my leg. I blurt out, 'Shit!' before I can stop myself.

'You've just insulted the *nats*,' heavy-breathes Dow Tip, coming up behind me.

'Bugger!'

I hit my forehead with the palm of my hand.

'And again,' he says.

Fuckitfuckitfuckit. The views from the top are lovely, anyway.

On the way back to Bagan, we pass a pickup crammed with people, with men only on the top.

'Don't the women like to ride on top? It looks fun,' I ask.

'They mustn't sit on top of trucks above men, because it is bad for the men underneath.'

'Why?'

'Women are inferior.'

I wonder what type of hell juice men imagine we are going to drip on them.

'I'm one of five boys, which is very good luck for a family. I have two girls and I want to stop having children but my wife won't let me until we have a son.'

'Why?'

'Because the gates of hell are shut against a person who has the merit of having had his son ordained as a monk.'

Dow Tip is a lovely, sincere, thoughtful man. But he has some strange ideas about women and menstruation.

'Why are there so few nuns?' I ask.

'Women cannot be nuns because they cannot meditate in the depths of the forest. When it's hot it's OK, but when it rains the girls fall down dead. The rain falls on their head and if they have blood inside, it becomes solid and a week later they die. The Burmese never ever pour water over their heads after being in the sun the way Europeans do,' he continues, 'because it breaks the nerves and they die.'

While I ponder this, Dow Tip lights himself a cigarette. Burmese cigarettes are named after long-distance glamorous places – Vegas, London, California – and are advertised with images of grainy, off-colour, seventies-style couples standing by a car, on a bridge, clearly about to be transported somewhere exotic and fulfilling.

'Are you angry?' he asks, inhaling.

'I suppose so, yes. Why do you ask?'

'Because of your reaction to the monkeys.'

'They hurt me!'

'Yes. Perhaps meditation would be good for you. It would calm your beating heart.'

'Not too much, I hope. A little beat is good for it.'

'What?'

'Nothing.'

'Of course women can't aspire to nirvana.'

'Of course not,' I reply, lifting my eyes to nirvana.

'When I was a monk I meditated every day for forty-five minutes each time. We weren't allowed to eat after noon, apart from jaggery, and we could smoke cigarettes. We went to bed at ten. We had breakfast at five in the morning but were up at two-thirty to wash and started meditating at three.'

'How awful.'

'Do you want to meet my teacher?'

'Absolutely.'

Dow Tip's teacher monk is called Yamaha and he

describes himself as 'a layer of cakes', but before being a monk he was a poet, 'which means I made pottery'. He speaks lots of English, but none of it makes any sense, it is one long meaningless string of words.

As we drive away, Dow Tip says, 'Would you discuss or follow?'

Discuss, definitely, but that's no problem as Yamaha is clearly in need of a good chat.

At the doctor's due to mild sunstroke, which manifests itself in headaches and shakes. The surgery is tiny with wooden benches and a plastic curtain separating the doctor's office from the waiting area, so everyone can hear what is going on. Old posters advertising condoms and garlic decorate the walls, but the place is bare. The doctor is a smiley man with dimples.

'Where do I get the medicine from, Doctor?'

'Here.'

I look around but most of the cupboards are empty.

'But, Doctor, you don't seem to have many medicines here.'

He smiles and sighs.

'I have to pay for most of the medicines myself. I can only afford cheap bad Chinese medicine.'

'Why are *you* paying for it?'

'Because the government does not give us any support,' he whispers, and checks outside the curtain to be sure no one can hear us.

'So they pay you?'

'Yes, I earn 300 kyat per month.' (That's just under 60p.) His smile is crooked, comprising irony, mild bitterness and acceptance all at once.

'Do you *have* to work for the government, though?'

'When you qualify you have to sign a bond that says you will work for the government for three years.'

'Oh.'

I feel helpless faced with these poor people.

'I'd better not get ill here then.'

Selfless to the end . . .

'No, try not!' he laughs. 'There are no medicines in the hospitals, and if there are they are this Chinese rubbish. You have to pay 50 kyat (10p) per day for your bed and buy all medicines on top of that.'

In the night I get up for the bathroom. Something large and scuttling is making its way around in there. I shut myself in with it, and consider various tactics. When I'm finished I open the door quickly to get myself out and keep it in there but the little bugger is waiting for exactly the same thing and hops into the bedroom with me. My reflex action is to bang the door shut against its body, shouting, 'Sorry, Buddha, sorry, Buddha,' as I do so, but somehow unable to stop banging the door until the vile thing is squashed dead. My heart beats loudly as I get back into bed, but a second later I get up for something else. I look down and, like a monster from a horror film, it is starting to pick itself up, brush itself off and move again. This time I absolutely smash it to smithereens. By the morning its body has gone. An army of ants has cleaned it away bit by bit in the night.

The barrage of insects could be one of the many reasons (the heat, jet lag, stomach upset) why I can't sleep. I am tortured by visions of decaying cadavers, women in black hovering over the bed, cockroaches scuttling over my legs.

It's not even ten and already the heat is cloying. Mainly because I'm on a bus to Mandalay. You can't really experience a country unless you take its local transport. At least that's the worthy-traveller bullshit I'm telling myself at the moment, though this is sheer hell, and if someone offered me a Lear jet I'd take it immediately, Buddhist or not. (Not. Have decided to postpone the meditation thing for a while.)

The bus is a shell of a bus. It's not even an old fifties American bus. It's one that got caught in a riot and was petrol-bombed, so stripped is it of any comfort. It stops every five minutes. When it does move, it honks at everything, *anything*, anywhere near it, drives much too fast through towns, near precipices, past children, and painfully slowly on long open roads. At one stage we drive alongside a train, cross the open tracks in front of it a few times, but in the end drive on ahead, which bears out the Burmese belief that taking the bus is always faster than the train.

At first there were little plastic stools down the central aisle, which I thought was a bit dangerous. Now there are two people per stool, about twenty on the roof and bodies hanging out of the door – it's like eighteen elephants in a Mini. The plethora of bodies leaning on me is sweaty and emanating an excruciating amount of heat. There are crates of tomatoes under my seat so my legs are tucked up under my chin. Still, to keep us happy, the driver has put on a tape playing the Asian version of 'Obladi, Oblada, life goes on . . . woah!' As for this bus-experience thing, the novelty wears off after five minutes. Which leaves another seven hours and fifty-five to go.

After a few hours and an Asian George Michael telling me he'll never dance again . . . I realise my bum is very numb, and clearly uncontrollable, as it is issuing its own careless whispers. I have to stop the bus, cross the road and use the facilities of the local café. As I am the only white tourist around, everyone (all men, the women are elsewhere working and keeping the country going) stares at me, laughing – and so does everyone on the bus. Hideously embarrassing. Still I don't care. I'm tired, filthy and very, *very* excited about never ever getting back on this bus again.

As soon as we pull into Mandalay's bus station, two boys buzz into the door, like gigantic alien flies invading the mother space ship in a sci-fi horror film, and announce my hotel. Expecting to be picked up, I squeak, 'Yes!' again, much to the amusement of my fellow passengers, and I follow one of the boys to – a trishaw.

I clamber in. Meandering behind black smoke-spewing buses for another forty-five minutes after eight hours on a bus is my idea of hell. I'm tired, filthy and sore. Suddenly an incredibly painful pellet is catapulted on to my back from the top of a passing local bus. My attacker is a novice monk. He laughs. At the hotel, the manager says he sent a car for me, so I could have arrived in comfort had I just waited a little. Then I pay my trishaw driver because it isn't his fault. And he has no teeth.

Finally up in a room, I put on my clean lungi and head out to find supper. The lungi is quite long and I trip up a couple of times. Women smile at my attempts to blend in – pretty pointless though considering how white and English I look. At least I hope they're smiling at my lungi. Or perhaps I have a bogey hanging from my nose? Personally I despise Westerners trying to be local. The white Hari Krishna monks with shaved heads and saffron robes, who chant and sprinkle flowers down Oxford Street, never fail to irritate me. Misfits one and all. I may be a misfit, but no need to advertise the fact. So I head back to the hotel to change into Western clothes. Unfortunately the second I step outside, I am doused in water thrown from the top floor of my very own hotel. Tomorrow is the start of Thingyan, the Water Festival. Some days one feels more of a twit than others.

8 p.m. The other travellers I see are couples and the lone travellers are always male. On the bus there was one guy in a green T-shirt who repeatedly refused to say hello even though the Burmese around us were gesturing as if to say, 'You two come from the same continent – why aren't you speaking?' But he had on this smug face that

said, 'I walk alone. I'm fine. I don't need conversation,' which terrifies off even the most over-friendly loser. Like me. So we're all trapped in these silly lonely little worlds. Well, I for one am desperate for a chat. Which is why I'm now encouraging debate and ridicule by sitting alone in the lobby of the hotel, hoping that that fifty-something perma-tanned American with long white ponytail and baggy tie-dye 'I've been on a kibbutz' trousers will come down and talk to me. I'm assuming that his advanced age will make him less hung up on this 'I'm fine!' thing.

9 p.m. OK. Where is he? Speculation as to what the hell I'm doing in the lobby watching telly by myself has now reached fever pitch amongst the rickshaw boys and the staff.

10 p.m. Back in my room. I was looking forward to spending a night in sheets rather than in my all-in-one sheet but sadly this is not to be. The amount of pubic hair in the bed and rat droppings on the pillow have made this a no-no. And yes I do know rat droppings when I see them.

10.15 p.m. For some company I turn on Channel Asia on the telly and watch a song about learning English:

> What is your ferret coler?
> She likes black just likes her hair.

I'm now repeating dance routines in front of the telly for my evening's entertainment.

10.30 p.m. Buddhism not going so well. I've just killed

more mosquitoes. Wondering whether to go to sleep when the decision is made for me – all lights go off, and so do the telly and air-conditioning.

2.00 a.m. Wake up when a cockroach runs over my inner thigh, heading upwards. Decide not to kill this one. Then spend the rest of the night wondering where on earth it is. I also ponder the impact of Buddhism on the Burmans' lives. When two bikes collide the one in the wrong doesn't apologise and the one who has every right to shout 'You. Filthy wretch. For crying out *loud* . . .' doesn't get angry. They merely disentangle themselves, brush themselves down and carry on. I wonder also if their concept of karma, the satisfying cause-and-effect theory whereby each life is influenced by the acts of the previous one, is the reason they accept the government and the human-rights abuses, figuring that they somehow deserve it from a past life. Then I remember that they did fight back, in their thousands throughout the country, but were brutally slaughtered in the massacre of 1988.

Just as I am simultaneously thinking this and wrestling with sleep, my mind blurs then focuses like a radio being tuned. Claudius is sitting at the end of my bed. I sit bolt upright.

'Kitkat? Is that you?'

'Who else is this good-looking?'

'Claude? Are you really there?'

I rub my eyes.

'You did call. So here I am.'

'Claw Claw?'

'Now stop repeating yourself. I'd like to tell you about the first cat. What do you say?'

'What? Yes. Why not. Absolutely.'

'Well, when the Buddha attained enlightenment under the Boddhi tree, the evil Mara, riding his war elephant Giri Mekhab –'

'Who?'

'Giri Mekhab, bearing the evil Mara, came down with an army of demons to give the Buddha the fear. But the Goddess of Earth, Nang Thoranee –'

'Who?'

'Nang Thoranee, squeezed waters from her hair to create a flood in which the demons drowned. Then Mara sent a plague of rats to eat the holy scriptures. So the Buddha created Phaka Waum.'

'Who?'

'Oh do stop saying that. Phaka Waum, the first cat, to kill the rats. That's how the first cat came about. And I need hardly tell you it is a great wrong to kill them,' he says importantly, yawning and straightening his back in a sitting stretch. 'It is in fact the equivalent of killing a *monk*.'

'Of course it is, Claude. No one's disputing that. But what about the story I heard?'

He looks bored, as he always did whenever I dared talk.

'Well, I heard that the cat was the only animal *not* to be blessed by the Buddha before he died because he was too *proud* and independent, and he therefore lost the Buddha's blessing, could never enter heaven and as a result is not the most revered of the earth's creatures.'

'Well, that tradition is *Chinese* for a start,' snaps Claudius. 'And of course the Buddha blessed the cat. Otherwise how else could cats have been so revered by the monks of this country for so long? Stealing a cat from a temple could result in death, for heaven's sake! Ordinary cats weren't allowed to mix with us, let alone mate with us!' says Claudius exasperatedly.

With that he curls into a tight ball, emits a few snores and is gone with a puff of brown smoke and a slight smell of burning.

Thais believe that if you dream of a cat it means money will be tight, friends scarce, and anger will abound. However, they also believe, as does the rest of the world, that if you see the *ghost* of a cat, you're bonkers. Either way, the prognosis isn't great.

SIX

MANDALAY TO MAYMIO

THE WATER FESTIVAL, in April, lasts for three days. It is also the start of the Burmese New Year. During these three days, the King of the *Nats*, Thagyamin, is said to visit the world and count the good and bad deeds of humans over the past year. He carries two books: one bound in gold to record the names of the good, and one in dog skin (not cat skin, mark you) for the bad. The Water Festival, unsurprisingly, is when the people celebrate water, and the best way they can do this is to pour it all over each other, in a symbolic cleansing of the past year's dirt and impurities. It is a welcome relief from the formidable heat, which continues until the rainy season in May. There is a saying that the people wait for the cicadas to throw water on the people then the people throw water on the people, because around that time of year, when you walk under a large tree, you get splattered by fairy-sized dots of water, from the cicadas above.

Day 1 of Thingyan
I walk out into the streets and seconds later so many buckets of water are poured over me that I almost choke from them. Standing at the bottom of the ocean would be a

drier experience. Unfortunately, today, for the first time since I've been here, it is not that warm. The result is that when I am wet – every minute of the day – my nipples stand out like machine guns, which I don't think is quite appropriate.

Much of Thingyan in Mandalay takes place around the moated fort. Most Burmese kings liked to start their reign with a fresh new capital, hence the glory periods of Bagan, Pegu, Ava, Amarapura and Mandalay, which was founded by King Mindon Min and was the last capital before the British colonised Burma. Mindon had the fort, or rather the walled palace, built in 1857. It was a city within a city. Apparently he had people (especially pregnant women) buried alive at the corners of the fortress and under the city gates in the belief that their ghosts would protect the inhabitants of the new city, though why they would want to do this, having been murdered by aforesaid inhabitants, seems unclear. In 1942 during fighting between the British, Indians and Japanese, the palace caught fire and burnt down. This was a common occurrence with Burmese buildings, which were generally made of wood. A new palace has recently been constructed, but I don't visit it because it was built using prison labour, and all entrance fees go to the government. This is the palace I believe the King of Burma says is always open to Princess Anne, should she ever want some Burmese hospitality.

By 10 a.m., the streets around the fort are crowded with cars and jeeps full of boys and girls made up to the nines, singing, dancing and shouting. Around the palace, stages have been set up, from which huge speakers blast out pop music. Privileged guests stand there with fire hoses, fed from the moat, and douse and soak anyone who goes anywhere near them. The road is a lake and the exhaust from the cars rises up to choke the throat.

I wander along, as jauntily as possible. Being alone at Thingyan is akin to being alone at Christmas. Everyone is in party mood, however, and soon I am surrounded by young men.

The first comes up and shouts, 'Which countlee you fom?'

I squeak, 'England!' my voice even more prep-school counties than before, to which the boy replies, 'Bootiful countlee!'

His friend behind him shakes my hand and asks, 'Which countlee you fom?' and I reply as before.

The next asks the same and so it goes on until every boy in the group has demonstrated his bootiful English and we have all smiled to our hearts' content. They move on to greet friends, have a dance, get a cool drink, get a good dousing perhaps.

I take one step and encounter another group of boys. 'Which countlee you fom?' and more hand-shaking.

After half an hour I am exhausted and wonder how the royal family copes. I have my 'I'm fine' smile on, but I feel as though I'm at my own funeral, surrounded by thousands of happy people.

Having a breather back at the hotel, I'm delighted, if surprised, to find the Yellow Pages. I flick through them to see if there is anything to do with cats in there. No, but there are other interesting sections such as 'Chilly Sauce' and 'Bags Gunny'. At lunch, I wander to the Mann restaurant, which is seconds away from the hotel. There is another tourist in there, but he is reading, and he has that look on his face, so I don't get excited.

After eating my revolting chicken-stew lunch (I really haven't got the hang of what to order and what not) the tourist comes over and sits opposite me! I can hardly contain my excitement! The words come tumbling out in my intense desire to talk! In proper English! Chad, American, from Virginia, travelling for three months so far, two weeks in Burma, lived in Japan for three years, doesn't like racist jokes, nice-looking, not boyfriend material, decent, sincere, sweet. Within seconds we have decided to travel together for a while.

We are staying at the same hotel so we go back to change before getting out there and trying the festival once again. I wait in the lobby – why do boys take so much longer than girls to get ready? He comes down dressed, to my horror, in his swimming trunks, and a floppy cloche-like sou'wester, looking more like a suburban teenager than a red-blooded Virginian.

Back at the fort, everyone is even more drenched than before, if that's possible. The boys are drunk. The girls are looking sullen and tired. The cars stop under each stage and have twenty hoses aimed at them. The pollution blackens the air. We walk through the calf-deep puddles, bits of mud, dirt, plastic, refuse, bogeys, spit (betel-chewing is rife at all times) and everything else flying in between our toes – we are all wearing flip-flops of course.

I don't like the fact but it's true – I sense that I am more acceptable due to Chad. He has legitimised me. I suppose I want to have my cake and eat it – be protected and yet be independent. Actually, why *can't* I have my cake and eat it?

We are invited to join several jeeps. We climb up and dance to the music with everyone else. Chad's dancing is true drongo-style – jumping up and down more monkey than human, but we all love it. He dances in the street with a boy who approaches him, they jump up and down in one another's arms, out of time, so that eventually the Burmese boy whacks Chad's chin with his head and Chad bites his tongue. The next guy gets a little over-excited and seems to be humping Chad's leg, but Chad doesn't mind one bit. Soon there's a string of boys, with lots of make-up and very tight T-shirts, giggling behind their hands, lining up to dance with Chad.

The boys are very respectful. The most they do is kiss my hand. I must have said hello to half the population of Mandalay. Chad keeps shouting 'Happy *Noo* Year,' like a New Yorker. As the day wears on, the cat in me starts to rise up and I realise that I hate, absolutely *loathe* being wet. And that I have two more days of this. Burmese girls and I smile sadly at each other. The men are getting drunker and drunker.

A guy comes up to me and says, 'You hev vagina.'

Just as I'm about to congratulate him on his biological

expertise, Chad steps in with a square-shouldered, tight-fisted, 'Watch it, Buddy,' and I quite like the squirmy, little-girl-protected feeling this engenders.

Chad is lovely, and yet quite strange. At one point when we're having a cup of tea outside a heaving café, he leans forward and *bumps* foreheads with me when I tell him a joke. (What does a dyslexic insomniac agnostic do at night? Lie awake wondering if there's a DOG.) He also calls me *hon* incessantly, which is no big deal, except I don't think I could put up with it for a long time. Except we're meant to be travel companions. I now realise that deciding to travel with someone after talking to them for five minutes is the travel equivalent of getting married after dating a guy for a week.

Day 2 of Thingyan

For a moment of peace this morning, I take to Mandalay Hill, for the classic tourist stroll. I get soaked on the way there, but once on the hill I am protected. Two-thirds of the way up I am somewhat startled by the image of the Buddha with a woman, whose chest is bleeding where her breasts should be. This is a depiction of the ogress Sanda Moke Khit, who was such a devout follower of the Buddha that she cut off her boobs as an offering to him. As a reward she was reincarnated as a man – and apparently was then reborn several centuries later as King Mindon himself.

I plonk myself in a café, called Chez Largo, and while contemplating just how far some women will go out of relief at finding a good man, I meet my first cat. At last! A Burmese

cat! Except she's a ginger-and-white mog, with half a tail and
a bald patch with a scab just behind her neck. She is quite
the ugliest cat I have ever seen, but I am so pleased to see
her, I buy half a chicken from the café and then feed her
it bit by bit. Overjoyed isn't the half of it. After a while her
pink-rimmed eyes gaze at me with true love. Then she sits
on my lap while I drink sweet thick condensed-milky tea.

Comforted by her presence, I daydream that all cats come
to see me to sort out their problems because I speak Cat. I
even speak Tiger and cavort with wild cats. It's your standard
'everyone loves me' fantasy, fuelled by fatigue and too much
condensed milk. Having seen so few cats, I wonder if she
might be my travelling companion from now on. When I
get up I'm almost vertical before she reluctantly realises I'm
not here for good. If she follows me to the loo, then I take
her with me, I think. But she doesn't. So that's that.

On the way back down, accompanied as usual by a
crowd of about thirty giggling boys, I am accosted by a
tiny shrivelled-up Indian.

'I spee Ingleesh. Yus!'

Hairs stick out of his ears at right-angles like a wild cat and
his head is topped by a grimy greasy turban.

'Ingleesh velly good! Fie Japanese 1945. I there! I fie with
English!'

He is referring to the battle when Mandalay Hill was taken
back from the Japanese by the British in 1945.

'You miss bes pah!'

He looks at my crowd of admirers venomously, then
stalks towards them like a cat. When close up he spews angry

Burmese at them, shooing them away, but they completely ignore him. In fact their numbers swell considerably as a result. He looks in turns shifty, nervy, then embarrassed.

He glances at the boys now and then, and finally announces toothlessly, 'Ingleesh velly goood, velly lucky, velly goood brain, Buhmeez bad.'

I sometimes forget that racism is not exclusive to whites.

He waves me to follow him, and we start back up the hill where he points out the standing Buddha, Shweyattaw, and the royal palace, behind which are reservoirs of water, the overcast city and the bluish Shan Hills in the distance.

'Boooodaaahhhhhhhhh!' he says right in my face. 'Boooodaaaahhhhhhh! Come here! Pledict 2,400 year of rain in grates of city.'

(I feel sure I've understood this wrong, but sure enough my guidebook later tells me the Buddha predicted that in the 2,400th year of his reign (1857 in our calendar) a great city would be built. Mandalay was founded in 1857.)

Back at the hotel, I bump into Chad. We wander out and have the most monumental water fight – us against Mandalay. Every tap in Mandalay is switched on, and most are accessed via hoses out into the street. Every bowl, every bucket, even shoes are used to cart the water from the tap to the back or head of anyone foolish enough to be passing by at that moment, whether they're on foot, on bike or in cars. The water is meant to be a blessing, and some Burmans, especially the girls, pour it gently and sweetly down your back while laughing. However, some are less friendly. The water they use is freezing cold and they thwack it in your face so that it stings, and some boys, now perilously drunk after yesterday, spray cheap perfume into your eyes.

It's back to the hotel for refuge, which has not been cleaned since we arrived and is getting filthier and filthier, the floors covered in wet mud as people come in sopping off the street. Unfortunately still one day left of the festival and because we are foreigners, we get soaked even more than everyone else.

Looking for something other than a good dousing, Chad and I go to the Moustache Brothers Puppet Show. The brothers are Burma's most famous travelling vaudeville group, famous not only in Burma, but documented worldwide, especially by Amnesty, as suffering one of Burma's many Human Rights Violations. U Par Par Lay, the elder brother, was sentenced to seven years' hard labour in Myitkyina prison camp (a prison for murderers and drug dealers, *not* political prisoners) after delivering one mild political joke at an Independence Day performance at Aung San Suu Kyi's residence in 1996. The other brother, Li Maw, keeps the tradition of *a-nyeint pwe* alive back at home in Mandalay, in order to make money to send food to his brother. *A-nyeint pwe* is a form of street entertainment, using dance, music, comedy and melodrama, suitable for any get-together, be it a wedding, funeral or celebration.

The show is performed in the tiny back room of Li Maw's puppet shop, which is open on to the street. Plenty of mosquitoes have come to watch too. We are given fans to wave them off. Soon the tiny room is blasting with cheroot smoke from the hippie travellers who think that smoking cheroots makes them a little Burmese.

Li Maw's show stars most of his family, whom he introduces one by one. His wife is the butt of most of his jokes, but she smiles along with us. He demonstrates each type of puppet, what princesses wear, what princes wear. We time him winding a cloth around his head to make the traditional male headdress.

He hands round his wife's dance book and we choose steps for her to do. Some of the travellers, especially a Swiss girl with toe rings, a nose ring, dreadlocks, a lungi around her floppy waist and a cheroot between her colourless lips, takes an inordinate amount of time poring over the tome until I'm itching to yell, 'For cryin' out *loud*! Just pick one! *Any* one!' but Li Maw is good-natured and smiles about everything.

His wife beats out a rhythm for herself with the words: *Toe perro pe toe perro pe* and then dances around the room in her tight long skirt. He explains what each movement of the dance is: holding gems up to the light to see if they're translucent, offering flowers to the king, looking at herself in the mirror to see if she looks good, checking to see if her lover is following her.

It is all harmless fun, though not helped by the slightly electric atmosphere thanks to the spy in the audience sent, every night without fail, by the police, to ensure Li Maw doesn't make any more political jokes. You might think that having a brother rotting away in jail would be enough to put him off joking for life, but he is the most positive, smiling, happy man I have ever met and I am impressed and humbled by the way he deals with his situation.

After the show in Li Maw's front room I strike up conversation with the Swiss girl. Her name is Maria.

'What did you think of the show?'

'Very lovely.'

She smiles sweetly, but reveals a stud on her tongue as she speaks, which from now, I can't help but focus on.

'And you?'

'I feel quite emotional, actually, considering how brave and smiling they are, in spite of everything they've been through.'

'Me too. The Burmese people always smile and laugh so much in spite of their poverty and lack of freedom. I wish I could get as much joy from my day as they do.'

We mmm in agreement and she introduces me to the Burman sitting on my other side who talks quietly in a thick Burmese accent.

We head back to our hotels. It's a surreal scene; we walk through the quiet dark streets of Mandalay late at night. Every now and then a whooping teenager pours a bucket of water over us, but engrossed in our conversation the Burman walks on, completely unruffled: the perfect manifestation of Buddhism – accepting what comes, trying to change nothing. Maria and I meanwhile are soaking and silently mouthing expletives to each other.

Every time I ask the Burman a question, he replies to Chad. I wonder whether Li Maw or his brother's wife have seen U Par Par Lay? He replies – to Chad – that no doubt they pray he is alive, since the conditions at Myitkyina are notoriously bad, with tortures perpetrated every day: the prisoners are made to crawl over sharp stones, or imitate helicopters and motorcycles. If they are not loud enough they get beaten. Their work involves breaking up stones for Myitkyina airport. They have to fill a truck an hour or they get beaten. They are fed watery soup. They have very little rest. They have irons attached to their legs which makes it hard to sleep. When they are ill they are left to starve in hospital, which is an official method of killing off opponents.

The Burman finally turns to Maria and me with kindly eyes and, as if we were his daughters, tries to cheer us up with tales of wicked wizard cats who have eyes of fire and black-grey bodies and who eat other cats, just leaving their heads. He says Burmans never buy cats – they are always a gift – and shows me tiny ginger kittens, covered in fleas, in the house opposite. But this is not enough to take my mind off proper human suffering a few blocks away.

Back at the hotel we retire to the bar/restaurant area. I chat to Maria while the men get the drinks.

She whispers, 'Are you going out with him?'

'*No!*' I whisper back. 'Actually he's a sweet guy but I don't really want to travel with him any more.'

'How long have you been travelling together?'

'A day and a half.'

'Oh. Well, why don't you tell him you'd prefer to be with a girl and tell him you're going to move on with me?'

'Excellent idea! Oh! And we'll then . . . ? Oh I see! Yes,

well, how lovely . . . I'd love to . . . oh aren't you sweet. Many thanks.'

Actually I don't want to travel with anyone at the moment. I seize the opportunity to tell Chad when he sits down that I'm thinking of travelling on with Maria, which is a mean way of doing it; but in a slightly irritating replay of my goodbye conversation with Matt, Chad doesn't mind at all.

Oh Lord.

I ask Maria if she has any scent I can borrow – I'm fed up with smelling. It occurs to me as I follow her dreadlocks and dirty lungi back to her room that she is perhaps not the best person to ask. But she tells me coyly to follow her. When we get there, instead of inviting me in to sample and spray, she turns to me meaningfully, and plants the wettest, slobberyest kiss on my lips.

'See you tomorrow then,' she says as she drops her eyelids, steps into her room and closes the door behind her as though she's playing hard to get, as though, 'No! I'm not the type of girl to sleep with you yet.'

I stand there for a few seconds, staring at her door in disbelief.

'I meant it about the scent actually,' I whisper to the door.

Day 3 of Thingyan
8 a.m. I'm on my way to Maymio because it's up in the hills, cooler and hopefully less frenetically Thingyan-orientated than Mandalay. And because there's a deluded Swiss hippie

back there. I'm in one of those pickup trucks, with two rows of open benches behind, on which the women sit. The men then pile themselves on the roof. I have somehow managed to get to the bus station without getting wet and now wait patiently (for two hours) in the cabin with the driver, terrified that Maria will come looking for me once she realises I've done a runner.

A lone European sits next to me. My new Buddhist philosophy means of course that I don't judge people by their looks, but he looks like the Angel of Death. His bright white legs reflect the light above yellow socks and sandals. His short shorts and tie-dye T-shirt are topped by sunken eyes, gappy teeth and blubbery lips.

We're up front with the driver so as not to get wet, but when we drive off the driver doesn't shut his window. A massive bucket comes in and we sit there soaked. I'm just about to turn to the driver and giggle when the other passenger turns to him and whacks him very hard on the forehead with the palm of his hand – a colonial with his slave. It is ugly ugly ugly and happens twice more as we drive out of Mandalay and wind up through the surrounding hills. The driver of course takes it as his karma and doesn't hold it against the European.

Pyin U Lwin, or Maymio as it was called from the 1880s by the British after a Colonel May, was the Brits' summer hill station. It is a lovely place to escape the dust and heat of the plains, being 1,070 metres above Mandalay. Lilac and mulberry trees surround large colonial houses with gardens of sweet peas, busy lizzies, dahlias and gladioli – a girlish riot of heavenly pink and purple. The air is cool. Painted, enclosed wagons pulled by horses are the local method of transport.

To avoid being soaked I spend a large part of the day in my new hotel with other travellers. Today we have: a nineteen-year-old New Zealander called Steve (he looks so young, all smooth, plump-skinned like a baby); two girls – one English (Mel) and the other French (Maxine); and a yowling cat somewhere in the garden.

Have solved the problem of personal smelliness with a string of jasmine around the neck at all times. How I would love a bottle of Chanel's Cristalle or some such materialistic invention of the West. But surely borrowing nail varnish from another traveller (Mel) is not against Buddhism? Hence the purple glittery varnish now on my toes.

While we paint our nails we swap travel stories. Mel is very positive and ballsy, and chats about the comprehensive she teaches at back in England, stories of mobile phones in classes and boys spitting at walls and girls dripping in gold jewellery swearing at her.

'Well, you've got to laugh, haven't you?' she says.

'Well,' I say when it's my turn. 'I saw a soothsayer in Yangon who told me I'd have an unfrightened goat. But I've worked it out and I think he meant a ghost that wasn't frightening. Because since I've been here, I've seen the spirit of my dead cat, and he wasn't frightening at all.'

Mel exchanges meaningful looks with Maxine. I feel slightly foolish.

The others quiz each other.

'How do you wake up in the mornings?'

'Oh I need three alarm clocks, and still I sleep right through.'

'Really? I'm like a light. Once I'm awake, bam, that's it, I'm up and running, ready to hit the road.'

'Really? Gee, I'm a sleepy dozy head in the mornings. My flatmate has to yell at me.'

'Not me, I'm . . .'

'I'm . . .'

'Me, I'm . . .'

'How much does a postcard cost here?'

'How much to send it or buy it?'

'Send it . . .'

'How long will it take to get to Hsipaw?'

'By train or by bus?'

'Both.'

'Well . . .'

'*So* what do you think is the geological make-up of this landscape?' asks Mel.

'Dunno. Solid toffee?' I reply.

'What?'

'Shall we have coffee?'

By the end my head is swimming with useless facts. The talk is like casual sex. Although fluent and fast, and therefore a strange relief in itself, it provides a false sense of security because we are in fact saying nothing.

'Why haar you travelling alone?' asks Maxine, her accent like treacle, her tone implying that there's something wrong with me.

'Because I want to,' I reply unsmilingly.

'We ev not met any buddy travelling alone,' she sniffs, looking away.

'Well, you're not missing that much,' I sniff back. 'They're either ridiculously stand-offish or overly randy.'

At which point a painted carriage draws up outside the hotel and Maria steps out, bedecked in silver jewellery and a top with tassels, her two chins wobbling, her toe rings gleaming in Jesus sandals. She drags behind her a long grubby brown sausage-type bag like a large brown poo.

'Maria! How lovely to see you!'

I brazen it out.

At which point she flounces past me, *à la* Sue Ellen, almost tripping me up with the sausage. When she's checked in, she comes out and joins us, and sits down next to me, much too close, but turns her back immediately and talks to the others.

'Did you get a Western toilet wiz yor rrrroom?' says Maxine.

'Oh I've been travelling so long I'm used to the squats.'

'And the squits,' I chime in, but get studiously ignored.

'Really the water system is great once you're used to it.'

I study her left hand warily.

'The Asians are much cleaner than us.'

'That's not hard,' I mutter.

After the preliminaries: why Maria's here (year off), how long she's been travelling (who cares), where she's been (Timbuctoo, the North Pole, Bognor Regis), where she's from (Cuckoo Clock Central), how long her toe-nails are (much too), what her favourite colour is (dappled Marmite), Maxine suggests we hire bikes and head for the Botanical Gardens on the other side of town. Mel stays behind to read and stay dry. At the bike shop Maxine and Steve haggle over 10 kyat with the owner for about half an hour.

'No, eez too much,' says Maxine.

Her hair is red. One of her eyebrows is shot through with a flash of white hair, like a fox.

'Please, my parents are in hospital,' says the owner desperately, his hands in the prayer position.

'Yayss. That's what they all say,' says Steve, trying to look authoritative, but a skim of insecurity whiffs off him as his squeaky voice hiccups over a dry swallow by mistake. 'No. We're not paying that.'

He shakes his head and looks at his feet.

'He's probably telling the truth,' says Maria, throwing me a twee look that says, 'Well, I *might* forgive you if you're *very* lucky.'

Finally they agree on a price and we cycle off, into the heart of Thingyan. By the time we arrive, we are soaked to the skin.

The Botanical Gardens have lovely flowers, but there is rubbish everywhere and crowds of people. Walking off to see some peonies, I sit on a bench and am suddenly surrounded by five Burmans, with a hosepipe. In a surreal tableau, they stand in front, dousing me with their pipe as I sit. This goes on for ten minutes. I'm intrigued to see if they get bored, but they don't. I ask if they might just stand apart so I can at least see the flowers while I enjoy my shower.

After a while I wander off to a lonelier corner of the gardens to a pond with a small bridge where a boy of fifteen greets me.

'Excuse me, madam, but I would like to practise my English. I hope I do not bother you.'

He tells me his name is Madonna ('But I not singer!') and then in beautiful careful English asks me my name, my age and my job (I lie) in scrupulously polite tones. He answers my questions about school and then tells me he wants to be a doctor later.

'But aren't the universities closed?'

'No, I have a place already at university in Yangon where I live.'

'Really? How?'

'I did the exams.'

'Well done. What does your mother do?'

'She is a nurse.'

'And . . . your father?'

'He is a general.'

'I see.'

He is charmingly shy with excellent manners. Perhaps it will be the next generation that changes the country.

Our tête-à-tête is interrupted by the approach of Maria. Her carefully applied *thanakha* paste is running down her chin, making her look sickly.

'Oh no,' I whisper under my breath.

'Is she your friend?' he asks.

'Sort of.'

'May I ask you a question, madam?'

'Please do.'

'Please do not take offence. But do Westerners ever wash? To us the people who travel around our country often seem very, very dirty.'

'They're not dirty,' I whisper. 'They're *filthy*! Darling! How lovely to see you! Must dash!' I holler and bounce off.

He looks baffled. She looks wounded.

As the sun sets I find the others, who are sitting near the edge of the gardens, looking somewhat miserable.

'Yayss,' Steve is saying. 'I've been haggling my way through Asia. I've saved myself a fortune.'

'*Oui*. Ozerwise zey tek you foh a ride,' says Maxine. 'Zey always trying to rip you off. My policy is beat zem down. It may only be a few kyat but it's zee principle zet counts!'

'Hmm,' I say, nodding my head and rubbing my chin thoughtfully. 'Remind me to file that under things I don't give a shit about.'

'What?'

'I said remind me to file that under things I must think about.'

'Oh.'

She throws me an evil look.

It's getting a little chilly so we head back to the hotel. Thingyan officially stops at 6 p.m., but as we wander up our street, almost dry, a young boy nips out from behind a tree and throws a bucket all over Maxine. Heh heh heh.

She goes berserk. She screeches her bike to a halt, turns it round, goes back to where he is standing staring in disbelief at the violence issuing from her mouth and wallops him incredibly hard around the head. He scuttles off clutching his head and looking as though he might cry. What is it with the Europeans thinking they can *hit* Southeast Asians?

'You cannot do this,' says Maria calmly, dragging hard on her cheroot. 'This their New Year. You cannot behave in this way.'

'It's after six o'clock.'

Maxine turns her wild eyes on Maria and I'm grateful she's not looking at me like that. Just then the yowling cat from the hotel walks past them, and stops yowling as its nose smells the air rife with vixen power-struggle tension.

'There's no law. And you are a guest in this country. Behave with some dignity. No Burman would ever be this way.'

'So what?' spits Maxine with venom, walking towards her. 'I'm not trying to be Burmese like you haar! I'm not trying to be someone elz! Look at you with your dirty clothes and your air which need a cot!'

'Ladeeez, please, let's keep calm,' says Steve, who looks terrified at this potential cat fight.

And then Maxine takes a swipe at Maria. And Maria ducks but wallops her back. Soon they are hanging off each other's hair, bitching at each other in French. It is thrilling in a ghastly way. And I wouldn't want to touch Maria's hair.

'Hey hey hey!' says Steve, tries to get in between them and then, '*Ow!*' as Maxine bites his hand.

Finally they spring off each other and stalk through the hotel gates, the cat just ahead of them.

'Look what the cat dragged in!' shouts Mel, rising up from a bench with her book. She then clocks the state of the two girls and frowns.

I join Mel for a gossip while the others go inside and clean up. As she walks away Maria looks at me mournfully with a 'Why weren't you my Prince in Shining Armour?' look. And I put my hands on my hips and give her a 'It's a big wide world out there. Make an effort to avoid me' look.

Scents of roses and lilac ride on the breeze, and songs of worship waft from a Christian church beyond the trees. Later as I shower, I decide to move on to Hsipaw first thing in the morning. I'd quite like never to see another traveller again.

SEVEN

MAYMIO TO HSIPAW

AT THE STATION, women sell provisions along the platform – cartons of wild strawberries, the speciality up in this region, delicious tiny nuggets of sweetness, hard-boiled eggs and bunches of flowers. There is a still in the air, with plenty of time to take milky tea in the café with its green wooden stools and tables; to watch the girl with straight black bottom-length hair languidly scratch her neck; to listen to the Indian music crashing through cracked loudspeakers; to watch the wagon drivers buy jasmine for their coaches, and hang it on the horses' harnesses before setting off; to haggle with the guy in the green knitted tank top decorated with a toy train on the right breast about the ticket price; to watch the people cycling across the weedy tracks; to breathe in the heat and dust.

When the train finally pulls into the station two hours late, the whole place comes to life with volcanic speed. Little boys and girls run up and down the platform with buckets and plastic cups shouting 'Aya-may-eh!' – 'Water available!'. Women sell sandwiches and large banana leaves containing steamed rice and spices. One woman is so worried she won't get on the train that the second it pulls into the station she heaves her enormous sack of food and provisions up on to the first step, even though a crowd of people are trying to get off.

At last we pull out of the station – and as we go, even though Thingyan is over, I get a full bucket in the face and on my nice clean shirt. Everyone in the coach laughs and I laugh too, but my mirth is bitter as unripe mulberries. Apparently, for the month after Thingyan, on the trains only, water is still thrown. It's strange because I seem to be the only one who got wet, but hey ho, the other passengers love it. There's a family opposite me, three women, one very old, and five children under the age of ten. They stare and then smile at me as I sit there dripping wet. When we stop at stations the train sways back and forth as though unsure whether to stop or not. The vendors come hurtling towards us with their baskets on their heads. Betel packets, red sticky cherry-like lollies, packets of sunflower seeds, slices of mango, chunks of coconut still in their milk.

The train is about to go over the Goktiek viaduct. The bridge was built over the Goktiek gorge by the Pennsylvania Steel Company in 1900, and at the time was the second highest railway bridge in the world. It connects Northeastern Burma with the rest of the country. Just before the pass we stop at a station where military soldiers get on board, make a beeline for me and make it clear that I am to take no pictures. Evidently there is a military camp near the bridge. The mournful horn sounds our departure. As we cross the bridge, I sit on the steps outside the doors. The train is almost in the clouds, the trees and valley stretching down for miles. We edge forward at a snail's pace, which doesn't inspire confidence in the bridge. The train curves and reveals other people hanging out of windows and doors for the splendid view. To my horror the woman from the seat next to me hangs her baby, naked, out of the window. 'Madam, no!' I'm about to scream, but she is just letting the baby pee, before whisking her back in. As she hangs her out over the abyss the baby emits a golden streamer, which breaks into a chandelier of topaz droplets.

Views of mountains with alopecia, the odd tree dotting here and there flits past the windows. These are the remains of the ancient forests whose logging has caused such environmental devastation. And there I was worrying about the jungle. There's hardly any left by the looks of things. Scores of yellow-and-white butterflies race alongside the train and further out are little piles of dried straw wigwams in yellow fields, tended by farmers with pointed hats who stop to wave at the train.

For the rest of the journey I am joined by a tarty Chinese woman, with bad skin and lots of white make-up. She sits opposite me with her legs apart, and one foot on the wooden seat next to me, chewing with her mouth open. She rarely takes her eyes off me, but is very friendly. She offers me her sweets and says 'Hsipaw?' regularly to which I nod vigorously.

Whenever the train gets up any speed, which is a rare and wonderful thing, it bounces up and down on the tracks so violently that the carriage doors swing open and we passengers become human Yo-Yos. Again the woman hangs her little one outside the train and I have images of a decapitated baby meeting the 5.15 Intercity from Glasgow coming in the other direction. But of course this is ridiculous. There is only one train a day and this goes so slowly, the child is more likely to be grown up by the time another passes.

Hsipaw is a Shan town. The last *sao pha* (prince), whose palace is still just about standing, was arrested in 1962 when Ne Win initiated his bloody stranglehold on the country, and hasn't been seen since. His wife, Inge Sargent, wrote a moving book, *Twilight over Burma: My Life as a Shan Princess*, about his disappearance and her subsequent flight from the country with her two young daughters. The *sao pha* was a liberal, reasonable, much-loved, enlightened ruler. He was no match for the blinkered, brutal, corrupt regime and most likely was shot within days of his arrest.

Hsipaw is a lovely small town with one main street lined with tamarind trees. I stop at one of the many B & Bs. The receptionist has a high squeaky laugh. When I ask him about cats he tells me of a boy who played with a cat and a week later it had turned up at his home, but had to cross a highway and river to get there and no one knew how it had done it. More evidence of the magic of cats. The guest house is clean and quiet. I have put all three of my clothes into the laundry and am alone without any of the travellers. So it's official. I'm thrilled to bits.

I ask the receptionist where I might find the best walk.

136

He points in the direction of the mountains to indicate the route.

'Very few trees,' I say, following the sweep of his arm.

'The trees were sold,' he says. 'What you cannot see has also been sold. The jade and stones are sold to the Chinese for weapons. China is eager to trade with us.'

'Many UK and US companies aren't, though,' I say hopefully.

'But this makes very little difference. With China trading with us, the generals have no fear of other sanctions. And China does not care about our human rights problems.'

'China's own human rights record is hardly laudable.'

'There is one European oil company which has stayed, and because of the lack of competition is set to make a fortune. But while they install their pipelines, huge amounts of trees are felled, animals killed and villages moved.'

The receptionist says this quietly, looking down as he fills in the ledger of the guest house. To outsiders we look as though we are discussing my accommodation needs for the oncoming days. He smiles.

'Of course what we need to do is educate our children so that they make changes in the future. The medicine and economics universities are open – but only for children of the government. Education is not for everyone. The government keeps saying it will open universities but it doesn't. Now where else are you going?'

'I'd like to go to Mogok. I believe it's near here.'

'It is, but that is closed to foreigners. You're only allowed to see the parts of Burma which look normal. You're on the tourist trail and Mogok is off it.'

I'm left to wander off, depressed, to lunch, where I am offered a choice of:

> sweed vegetable
> chicken with sora bean past
> pork skin toast
> fired sausage with mustered and spirach
> fried arsdine

Well, it all sounds delicious, but somehow I've lost my appetite.

That night I watch Arsenal play Leeds at the local cinema. There are no lights because the generator broke down a month ago and hasn't been fixed yet so Hsipaw is lit up at night by candlelight. Women line the roads, squatting by grape-filled baskets with a candle dripping in the middle. It is beautiful to me, though no doubt less charming to the locals who must be sick of it by now. The spectators yell for both sides, so I am confused as to who to support.

The first time I saw Arsenal play, with Matt, my erstwhile boyfriend, my blood ran cold when a player fell over and didn't move. He's dead, I thought. Typical. My first match and someone dies. He was carried off on a stretcher but five minutes later came bounding back like a puppy, all trace of agony disappeared.

The Burmese love the high drama, hysterics and hypo-chondria. They shout and spit betel juice constantly. I just sit there thinking: Men. Tuh!

Next day I go for a walk. I am joined by a thousand butter-flies, lilac flutterbies, yellowy-green-and-white buttermyeyes, black-with-white-marking flutterhighs. They seem to be the only life-force allowed to flourish in this country. I walk along the railway track for miles, past mounds of rubbish left by pilgrims, past scents of wild mint and shy-lady flowers, picked by boys wearing pointed bamboo hats and riding bikes, past fields of rice and soya and the odd teak tree with mountains in the distance.

Finally I get to a Shan village, to a bamboo house where the women are sitting on the floor working. One is making multicoloured bamboo fans, to sell at the market. Another is making bamboo thatch, weaving leaves in and out with deft fingers. Another is pulling the wings off cicadas. These are caught by young boys by means of a sugar-coated long stick, which they position carefully in the trees. The father of the house brings out a bowl of fried cicadas for me to eat, and I look up, concerned, into his smiling, toothless face. I put one gingerly in my mouth. It tastes of ginger and salt. Once over the horror of putting such a large insect in my mouth, I'm struck by how delicious it is and shovel more in.

The family tells me stories of rice. Bags of rice cost 8,500 kyat (£16.80) but they are forced to sell 10 per cent of their rice to the government at 1,300 kyat (£2.60).

139

Shan rice is the best but they often don't have enough to feed their families, so they sell theirs, as they are forced to, and then buy back worse-quality rice from Mandalay merchants. Government agents have come up and told them to grow corn. The climate and soil are not suitable – the tiny stunted corns in the market are proof of this – but still they are forced to buy corn seed at vastly inflated prices. This family had to sell their buffalo in order to do this, which means they had to give rice away to another farmer to hire his buffalo. They then didn't have enough rice to give the government their 10 per cent stake, so they were forced to pay interest on the money the government had given them for that 10 per cent. If the village as a whole is unable to give the government the amount of rice it wants, the village headman has to send boys to the army – a neat means of forced recruitment. The government doesn't care if the ground is unsuitable for the crop, the man says angrily, they just want money, and if we can't buy their seed then we go to prison. And the same with the fertilisers. Chemicals are sold in the market for 2,000 kyat (£3.96) but the government shops sell it at 3,000 kyat (£6) and the family have to buy from there.

I ask the father if he wishes to know anything about life in the West. He says yes. But unable to remember anything else, I talk about celebrity prenuptial agreements, the usual stuff rice farmers who don't have enough to eat all year round are simply dying to hear about. I walk away feeling like a complete and utter idiot.

I continue my walk past a village with very pretty houses

on stilts. The houses have walls of bamboo leaves, thatched roofs, bamboo shutters, bamboo-pole fences around tidy yards, bamboo bicycle sheds, even bamboo cradles. I almost expect to see bamboo cars to be parked in bamboo garages. They are a cross between something out of *The Flintstones* and something out of *Homes & Gardens*. Someone must be friendly with the government in here, because the place reeks of a primitive prosperity.

I cross stone bridges and walk between lush green rice fields, on raised mud walkways curving towards the spires of the Mahamyatmuni Paya, Hsipaw's most important religious site, in the distance. The sky is thickening with grey heat.

Back in town the evil karaoke shops blast out the musical equivalent of sick. Why are Southeast Asians so nuts about karaoke? And why are the people who adore karaoke usually the ones who really can't sing? Listening to the whines and groans of army boys on their outpass, I could be in the middle of summertime Ibiza, but no, I have to remind myself that actually I'm in the depths of Burma.

Outside one bar a group of soldiers is circling a girl and taunting her. Her long thick black plait swings down her straight back as she turns this way and that. She bares her white teeth, which contrast with her smooth *cappuccino* skin and chocolate-brown eyes. She looks scared and on the verge of tears. They are poking her in the ribs and she thrashes about like a fish in a net. The boys are clearly drunk, swigging away at Myanmar-beer bottles.

I'm enraged and start hoofing towards them shouting '*Hey!*'. Two of them eye me coldly – they're clearly not used to being reprimanded. As I walk past a tiny shop an old woman holds out her hand and stops me. Her grip is strong – she holds me back. Two of the boys – they're not much more than sixteen – swagger over, an ugly glint in their eyes. She starts babbling at them, smiling, her hand shooing them away. 'Go back to your fun!' she must be saying. 'It's all right, she's just a foreigner with their funny ideas.' They give me filthy looks, their mouths turned way down at the corners, and the younger of the two spits betel on to my foot – disgusting. I'm about to knock his block off but the woman drags me into her shop and in perfect English tells me to calm down and leave well alone.

'But they're hurting that girl!'

'No, her father has just stepped in. He will pay them a fine and then there'll be peace again.'

'What? Pay *them* a fine for mistreating *his* daughter?'

'Don't worry yourself. Don't worry yourself.'

She whispers, looking around nervously, aware by now that her protecting me will have done her no good at all.

'They're just nasty army thugs. They're illiterate, uneducated boys recruited from the villages. They've been brainwashed. When they're recruited they go to Lashio for a year and are sent far away from their homes. They are taught to care only for the government and not for the people. That's why they behave like this. You are fighting against mind games. So no chance. What you were going to do would have ended up very badly for you.'

'But what about their religion and their upbringing? Don't they know what is happening to this country? Why do they join the army?'

'Food and shelter,' she whispers. 'But it is a poor exchange. Once in, they cannot leave. If an officer wants to retire he must find six or seven boys to replace him, which of course is impossible. They cannot return home and have no holiday. If they escape they are very severely punished. Of course the military intelligence is very loyal to Ne Win – they live very comfortably. There used to be just 150,000 in the army. Now there are closer to 500,000. They want to threaten the people and rule for ever.'

She looks up and the two army boys are back. They evidently don't speak English because they shout questions at her and she replies rapidly, still smiling. Their exchange continues until she puts her hand in a box and gives them each some money, plus a couple of betel packets. They sneer, turn and go.

'What did you do?'

'They wanted to know why we were friends. I said you had just come to buy some sweets and were a good customer.'

'And the money?'

'They said I shouldn't be exchanging ideas with foreigners, that foreigners had nothing good to give. I knew it was a hint so I tipped them, with the money from your sweets.'

'But I didn't . . . Oh I'm so sorry, please let me reimburse you.'

'Oh no, no, please no. This is the Shan way, you are my guest and very welcome.'

'Absolutely not. I must reimburse you. Really.'

I hold out money but she won't take it. In fact the longer I'm there the more trouble I cause her. The army boys are still malingering in the street and looking over occasionally. I stuff a few notes in her box and run out.

'I'm so sorry for causing you trouble,' I whisper over my shoulder.

Back at the B & B, I find it is packed with travellers, all in on today's train. Mel is there. So is the ghastly Maxine. All talking about prices and train timetables and lengths of journeys.

Today, once I'm sure there are no army boys around, I go back to the old betel woman, name of Mala. She has the brightest eyes and most smiling face. In the corner of her store are bundles of clothes to give to the poor. We wander around the market together, weaving in and out of women with baskets full of tiny garlics, ginger, carrots, melons, cabbages, beans, dried fish, eggs, tomatoes, greens and cicadas. They all carry their goods in the typical Shan shoulder bags – multicoloured with long tassels hanging off the bottom, and very long shoulder straps. Even men carry these bags. The cicadas seem to be moving still, but on closer inspection are in fact just swarming with flies. She shows me the best noodle stall and we eat sticky noodles together. I tell her about my search for the perfect cat. Back at her house she prepares a package of food.

'May I ask you something, Mala? Is there any way I can get to Mogok?'

'No. It's closed to foreigners. And you don't look at all Burmese. Why don't you go to the Mahamyatmuni Paya and pray instead? But I must say goodbye for the day,' she says. 'I'm going to see my daughter.'

'So sweet. You're taking her food. My mother used to bring me food too.'

'Ah, I have to. If I didn't she would not eat.'

'Why not? Is she anorexic?'

I regret this the second it has slipped out.

'No, she's a teacher. But after she trained she couldn't get a job. I had to bribe the government official to secure the job for her, and he is taking her first three months' salary. You see, this is how the government works. Children and relatives of government officials get the jobs they want regardless of whether they are qualified or not. Then whoever has bribe money gets the job. Businessmen have to bribe to get their licences – they are always having to donate money to the government and attend self-congratulatory ceremonies to show their support.'

'And where is your daughter now?'

'Miles and miles away up in a tiny village in the mountains.'

'Couldn't she get transferred back here?'

'Normally teachers only stay in jobs far away from home for two years. But she has been allocated a school in this village for five years.'

'How awful.'

'This is our country. This is how it is run now. Restrictions. Corruption. Even some of the monks are corrupt.'

'What?'

'The government puts their own monks in the temples, because they have such a powerful influence on the people. But I must start my journey. It will take many hours and I have not been for a week. But I forgot to tell you. I saw a very big brown cat with green eyes around here last night. I will keep an eye out for it when I come back, but I think it is what you are looking for.'

Excitement unparalleled.

The heat, the heat, the heat. There is no escape from this parchment, this crematorium, this fiery battle ground. Wandering around town much later, I meander to the Mahamyatmuni Paya. Here the most bounteous offering has been made by two very rich families. There are numerous huge sacks of rice and bags of onions, soaps and toothpaste and fans and brooms and hats and everything you could wish for materially, although ironically these are all for the monks. It is the custom to make offerings just after Thingyan.

If I lived in this country, I'd become a monk. I'd neither work nor worry about money, but instead would pray and think higher thoughts, learning how not to get wound up by the government. I must learn some higher thoughts. I must be as serene as Claudius. And try not to get too excited about Mala's brown cat.

EIGHT

HSIPAW TO INLE LAKE

IT'S THE FULL moon. This morning at five I hear chanting and singing. Wondering if it's a *pwe* that will take me to the heart of the people, I slip out of the guest house and walk into town, following the singing, the chanting that flies on the wind. It is quite light, musty, fresh. As the mist lifts and the blue-grey light gives way to gold, dark figures take on the shape of people, gathering ready for another day's market. Shan women set out their produce, rhubarb stalks and bananas, bunches of flowers and salad leaves. The singing is sometimes ahead of me, sometimes behind, but I can't find it. For a moment it occurs to me that it could be from last night's Juventus v. InterMilan match but then a small scuttling man tells me it's the monks, who will keep chanting for a hundred hours. Disappointed not to come across whooping, naked, dancing, celebrating *nat* worshippers, I head back to bed.

Later I wander to the *paya* where there is an enormous lunch. When the hosts notice me spying on the proceedings, instead of shooing me away with a broom, which is what my strange behaviour rather deserves, they immediately bustle me over to a low table. I sit cross-legged and am served the most delicious lamb curry, in a succulent, oily, cucumbery sauce, with rice, crackers and a spicy soup. Women in their finery are seated at various tables. They feed their babies and play with their little children. The girls are dressed in spangly shiny princess dresses and have sparkly tiaras on their tiny heads. Men lounge smoking at separate tables. Pudding, a bowl of coconut ice-cream, tea, sesame seeds and nuts, is served at low tables in the next room. The server bends in respect as she walks past elderly people. Loud music with chanting blares from huge speakers at the corner of the *paya*. People stare at me but smile.

Afterwards I thank the head monk. He looks about twenty but assures me he is fifty. Perhaps meditation is the secret of eternal yoof. He explains that this is a *shin pyu* – a novitiation ceremony – paid for by three families from Mandalay. That three young sons are about to enter the monastery for the first time. They will form a procession through town and once at the monastery they will have their heads and eyebrows shaved, the hair caught in a special sheet, their finery removed, and tomorrow morning they will take to the streets with an alms bowl to beg for their food like the Buddha.

Sure enough a procession forms once everyone has eaten. Three boys, looking remarkably like girls, in white trousers and pink satin jackets and gold-sequinned fez hats, are carried on the shoulders of their fathers under parasols all around the *paya*. Their feet are not allowed to touch the ground, as they symbolise Prince Siddharta before he renounced his life of luxury. Their faces are made up with rosy blusher and red lipstick so that they look like dolls. Behind them is an enormous crowd of children and adults clapping and singing and musicians walking at the back. The procession is headed by women in white shirts and brown skirts and pointy bamboo hats who clash cymbals and bang drums. They are followed by other women in their most colourful finery carrying flowers and fans.

The procession works its way around the temple, down the covered pathway to the street, where the boys are put on ponies and led through town. As they proceed more and more people join them until the entire town empties itself. They stop at various houses – where the boys pay respect to older members of their family and receive donations before they renounce the material world.

Suddenly a woman throws sweets to the children, like grain to chickens, and as her arm spreads so does her thick black sheet of shiny hair like a peacock tail down her back. The children go wild as they see her. The sweets soar into the air and then scatter helter-skelter along the floor like stones scudding water. At the back near the musicians is a group of beautiful boys dancing in a circle surrounded by clapping friends. They dance in the traditional way, turning their wrists and ankles out, looking somewhat effeminate as they do. When they smile their teeth glisten red from recently chewed betel.

When the procession reaches the monastery, everyone halts, because an elephant is in the road. The elephant then crosses its legs and moonwalks – highlighting the possibility that it is in fact two men dressed up. My shock at its not being real brings forth cascades of laughter from everyone around. The elephant then bows three times to the children before letting them pass. This signifies the animals coming to worship Buddha.

The head monk about to receive the boys is called Sin Maw. He is surrounded by young monks with shaved heads, dressed in their burgundy robes, one shoulder bare, like mini Roman emperors. Some of them play football in the yard. The sweetest are the tiny little tots, not more than three years old, in specially designed robes, which have a piece of cloth over the shoulder buttoned to the bottom skirt, as they are too little to understand the folding of the robes.

Much later, after the ceremony, when everything has calmed down, figuring I've been brought to this place for a reason, I ask Sin Maw to help me meditate. We take off our shoes, and climb the steps of the shrine, which is at the top of a small hill, has no walls and looks out to the fields. I face myself towards the golden spire at one of the corners and sit in the lotus position. Sin Maw talks me through my first meditation, explaining that I'm not to move at all but should empty my mind. He says that all pain will eventually go away, and this seems a good thing to learn. He's then silent for what seems like seven hours but is in fact twenty minutes.

When he tells me to wake up, my legs are so numb I can't walk on them. I follow him down to the monastery and sit at his feet while we discuss Buddhism. I find it all slightly confusing and very passive (if you see your mother being beaten up you're meant not to interfere as she is paying for a sin from her past life and you'd be interrupting the order of things) . . .

After an hour, we go back to the shrine to meditate again. Sin Maw leaves me up there, my legs crossed, my bag next to me. I meditate and all I can think of is how hungry I am, how painful my joints are and how I can't wait to stop meditating. When I open my eyes, my bag is open – and my purse is gone. Stolen! Of all the places . . .

Pretty soon the entire monastery is up in arms. Several boys run off in the direction of the village after the thief – as they all know who it was. The head monk presides over a big conference with everyone putting in their ha'penny worth. There's great excitement. My credit card was in there but this is not a problem as credit cards are useless in Burma. There was some cash. And my aeroplane ticket. For once I have left my passport at the hotel. The monks then offer me food. They feel guilty. It's exquisite – rice, meat and general deliciousness – but Sin Maw is annoyed with me.

'Why did you leave the bag by itself?' he asks.

'Because I thought it was a sheer drop the other side, and because this is a monastery! I didn't realise real life impinged in here,' which is no doubt a thick thing to say. 'Anyway. As long as the thief doesn't spend the money howling away at a karaoke bar.'

'Oh I don't think he will.'

He then turns to the others and they discuss the likelihood of the karaoke bars, until dazed and bemused looks surface in my direction.

'Joke, Sin, joke,' I mutter under my breath.

To take our minds off the situation we watch some novices being given bowls and robes. Amongst candles as the light is now fading, the monks pray and chant over them, while the boys are helped into their robes by other monks. The tiniest gets hold of another novice's robe and walks around with it on his head like a little brown ghost until he is swooped up by another monk and put into position again.

Just then the superior arrives on a motorbike with the thief, a boy of about seven or eight. They lead him to the chief monk's lodge and we all sit on the floor. The boy is terrified. He's thrown the purse away. I get my money back but no credit card and no aeroplane ticket. He holds his hands in a *wai*, and looks about to cry. After a while two thick tears roll down his cheeks. The monks say he's fourteen. He's the smallest, most undernourished fourteen-year-old I've ever seen. He's questioned and in a whisper he tells how his father has never given him any money, so he has worked by roadsides and then in a teashop but was dismissed because of his thieving.

'We keep him here over night,' says Sin Maw.

'Don't punish him too much, please.'

'He must learn not to do it again. But don't worry – we will find your purse tomorrow and the credit card and I'll give it to another traveller to bring to you in Yangon.'

I have visions of Maxine getting her dirty mitts on my credit card and paying her way around Southeast Asia.

'*No!* Sin Maw, promise me, *never!*'

I don't know whether they're talking about the incident because they're embarrassed and think they should address it as long as I'm there, or because they're kind, but I want us all to forget it, so I leave.

A strange day today. I take a bus out of town to the hot springs. I haven't a clue where to get off – and it is weird being carried fast into the unknown, unsure whether I'll get back. The driver tells me my stop and I walk in the thumping heat past fields and towards a village. I ask about springs in very bad Burmese and the odd person I bump into has absolutely no idea what I'm talking about. I eventually find some concrete tubs and dip in them. A boiling bath under the boiling sun is not the best idea. Though I would say from the horrified look on the locals' faces that I might just be bathing in the village's drinking-water tank.

I then hitch to Bawgyo Paya, a most revered site containing four gold Buddha images and many pillars covered in coloured-glass mosaics. Very few people are here, just a couple of girls wearing lots of gold jewellery and a man. I walk to Bawgyo village – because there's only so much nodding you can do – but the sun is intense.

I turn back and hitch instead to the cemetery of the Shan princes. This involves hiking up a hill over scratchy scrubland to a shell of a place, overgrown like the Sleeping

Beauty's castle, with thick angry briars all over the mau-
soleum, which has completely reverted to nature. The
authorities clearly don't want it remembered. The stillness
makes me extremely sad for this country, for what it used
to be and what it has become. It's a melancholy, lonely
morning where I'm never really sure what I'm doing. The
only comfort are the poinciana – red-flame trees – along
the roads as I hitch back into town to Mala.

Mala proudly shows me the brown cat in her lap. I have
never seen a more ginger cat in my life. How she could ever
have thought it was brown, I do not know. Marmalade cats
are lovely but no substitute for Claude.

'Well then, you must go to Inle!' she smiles.

'Why?'

'Because there is a monastery there with lots of cats.
They jump! They're jumping cats.'

'Are you sure?'

'Of course.'

Well, why not? It's not as though I've been overcome
by the choice of cats available here.

Inle, here I come.

NINE

INLE LAKE TO KALAW

THE JOURNEY TO Inle is by bus, leaving at six in the morning. Mala waves me off, and I am sorry to go. On the bus there are crates where my legs should be, meaning I sit for ten hours with my knees under my chin. My bum is numb before the bus has even moved. The earth turns red and the road hairpins like Scalextric tracks tighter and tighter. We wind down the mountains, cross a river, and then back up again into more mountains. The mist rises.

At lunchtime the bus stops at a restaurant, near which salted damsons, masses and masses of them all over the pavements, are laid out to dry. I try not to step over those spilt out into the road, in a Burmese version of avoiding the lines in case of bears.

'Are you superstitious?' asks a fellow passenger, a Burman with eyes like stitched-in black buttons.

'No. Yes. Sort of. Are you?' I reply.

'I see an astrologer regularly. This is very important for us.'

'I know.'

'Do you? Do you know how important?'

'What do you mean?'

'Ne Win consults astrologers all the time to choose auspicious dates.'

He pauses and looks around to see if we are being overheard.

'Ne Win was born on the 18th of September and as a result he likes the number nine.'

'Yes?'

'He announced the Visit Myanmar Year on the 18th of November, 1996.'

'I don't understand.'

'1+8=9. November is the eleventh month. 1996+11 = 2007. 2+7=9.'

'Oh.'

Nutty nutty nutty. *Anyway*.

'Does he use astrologers for everything?'

'Well, an astrologer once told him that he had to bring the country round more to the right. He wasn't pleased with this because he was heading more to the left, towards greater socialism. So he took it literally and made everyone drive on the right-hand side of the road. Of course we had driven on the left since the British went.'

'And what about the grand election?'

'He chose the 27th of May, 1990 because he liked the number 9 in the date. The farmers weren't happy though because it fell in the middle of the growth of their second crop, making it very difficult for them to get to a voting station.'

'Perhaps that was the point. What else does he do?'

'He got rid of the old banknotes, the 25, 35 and 75 kyat

notes, in 1987 without compensation. This wiped out the savings of the middle classes overnight. He also introduced 45 kyat and 90 kyat notes because they're multiples of 9.'

'How strange to make your own people poor.'

'Not everyone's poor. The property and belongings were confiscated from the Trade Minister by the generals who thought he was too soft on the people. He owned 9 tonnes of gold bars, 6,000 million kyat, inestimable jewellery and eighteen luxury cars.'

'But the King of Burma told me the generals earn a normal salary.'

'Who is this king?'

'Don't you know? He's the pretender to the throne.'

'Really? I've never heard of him.'

'Perhaps that general was different from the others?'

'I don't think so. The Minister for Tourism and Border Trading had to give up two enormous compounds with 6 tonnes of gold bars, twelve luxury cars and enormous amounts of jade.'

My companion and I chat for the rest of the journey. Burmans who talk to foreigners often want the world to know what is happening in Burma, hence the heavy amount of information in a short meeting. He tells me more about the 1990 election. Ne Win's party had twenty months to canvass and organise themselves. He gave the opposition NLD one month in which to visit every village in each township. If they went to a village they had to report to the commission office, immigration and

Military Intelligence. They were told not to criticise the government but just to tell the people to cast their votes. In one community, only one week before the election, the commission office called the NLD leaders and told them to proceed to the commission office where three-star military officers were to meet them.

They were told to arrive at nine, which they did, only to have to wait two hours for the officers to arrive. They were then told that to qualify as leaders, they had to have parents and grandparents who were born in the area and they must not have had any contact with foreigners. The officers then gave them a piece of paper with the names of fifty villages on it.

'We can't give proper security to these villages so they have been excluded from the election,' they said.

'But the local rebel armies have made peace with the government, and most of the villages are roadside trading villages with polling stations anyway. So why is security even an issue?' the leaders asked to no avail.

The remaining villages in that township had an uneducated, illiterate populace who were easily led by the village headmen, who would ensure they voted for the government.

The leaders left and found a tape from Aung San Suu Kyi back at their headquarters. The village headmen would not allow them to address the villages. So that night they gathered at a secret house and spent all night making copies of the tape. Next day they played the tape to a less important village headman. He was won over by Aung San

Suu Kyi and made his village listen to the tape. Over the next six days they arranged for all the villages to hear it. The NLD won. But it made no difference. Aung San Suu Kyi was forbidden to hold her weekend meetings outside her compound and the election results were ignored.

'Ah! The boys play *chinlon*!' says my companion suddenly – pointing outside the bus to a circle of boys, dressed in nothing but their lungis tied up under their crotches to reveal short muscly legs.

'They must keep it in the air but not touch it with their arms or hands. Do you know this game?'

'Yes, it's a form of hackysack,' I reply sadly, my mind still on what he's just told me.

One boy bounces the ball up in the air a few times and then tosses it on to the next boy. It's a strangely carefree moment, in complete contrast to the repression I've been hearing about, but yet not carefree enough to cool the depressing after-taste of the story.

Travelling alone is about taking risks – mainly with people. After my eight-hour bus ride to Mandalay, I meander towards a restaurant. On the way, a boy hurries up to me. He says more than just 'I luff yoo, where do you go?', he says, 'Princess Diana millions crying September 15th, 1997 her funeral I know it her two son Hanny Wilyum you very kind you travelling many places Paris France Italy I speaking French language, *allez-vous ciao* that's in Italy I know it.'

Even though his constant protruding and withdrawing

his neck like a woodpecker, bulging his eyes till they are golf balls, and alternately sticking his chin and goofy teeth out ease him firmly into the pigeon-hole marked 'nutter', I invite him to supper.

'Australia, San Francisco, Chickaggo, Humerricah, Kanadar, Netherlands – you know them? I like the music – Fleddy Mercury she dead sick years hago, I like it, ACDC, Australia, Michael Jackson. We are the world. I like it. I know.'

He then speaks to the waiter in English. The waiter doesn't understand a word. The obvious thing would be for him to revert to Burmese, but he chooses not to. After five minutes of negotiating, I'm so hungry and tired I don't care what they bring and I let them decide for me. This is why I always seem to be eating snot sauce. Finally my new companion turns to me and stares hard.

'You very good friend. Very close friend. I want souvenir. You come to photo booth with me.'

'I'm tired. I just came out to eat and then I'm going to sleep.'

'You very kind to me.'

'No. No, I'm not.'

'Yes, I go there with my family too. Holiday. Where do you go?'

'Inle Lake.'

'Why?'

'Because I understand there are jumping cats there.'

'From where?'

'The cats?'

'No you from where?'

'London?'

'*No!* You come from where?'

'Maymio?'

'You go to Maymio tomorrow?'

'No. I've come *from* there.'

'You go to Maymio after Inle?'

'*No*. I've been there already.'

'What music?'

'Madonna.'

'I like he! He black woman! He wear red leggings! Yes I know it. I read *Newsweek*.'

'*Newsweek* from another planet perhaps if that's the information they're feeding you.'

I'm impressed by his determination to learn English without the help of school so I speak pidgin with him.

'After school, what you do?'

'Nothing.'

'Oh. What you job?'

'Nothing.'

'You no bored?'

'No, I'm not poor.'

'How do you live?'

'I take money off my mother.'

'What does she do?'

'Make jewellery.'

'Do you want a job?'

'I lazy. I not know any idea what to do.'

'You could be a waiter?'

'Waiter!'

'No! Shush. I mean you could be a waiter while you decide what you want to do.'

'Waiter!'

'*No!*'

'No, I not proud. They don't talk to you. How ages are you? You hansum woman. Not old woman with backpack. Glasses. Look. Hat. I see.'

'Er, thank you.'

For pudding he orders *crème caramel* which reacts weirdly with his saliva, causing tiny white droplets to spew all over his lips and teeth. He also talks non stop while he eats, giving me direct viewing-access to the white watery mess inside.

'Yes, I like Queen vell mush. Many peoples like Queen. Very popular. And Doctor Marten shoe. In America. FBI. FBI.'

He repeats FBI like a stuck needle for about three minutes.

'Federal Bureau Investigation and scare. Yes I know. CIA. CIA. CIA.' Ditto. 'America only. CIA. I know it. Pin Floy. Another blick in ha woll. Michael Jackson was black man. Now compooter on face. Make hup whaat. You velly good flen. Thanjew fo more.'

Help.

Another eight-hour bus to Inle Lake. Finally I arrive at Nyaungshwe, the little town just north of the lake. The first room my hotel shows me has a moving floor, until we turn on the lights and see cockroaches scattering to the ends of the earth. I'm upgraded to insect-free rooms.

This morning a greying fifties English couple next to me order their breakfast.

The man says composedly, 'I don't suppose you do a poached egg, do you?'

There is a pause while the girl looks at him as if he's asked her to Morris dance.

Then with a patronising smile, 'No. I suppose not.'

I am out on the calm lake motoring towards the floating market and other villages situated around, forming a Burmese Venice. Above me egrets fly in formation towards – who knows where? – the marsh lands and hills in the distance. Below me the water is clear and very shallow. Beside, dragon-flies take turns to fly along in accompaniment. The people of Inle Lake are the Intha, who local folklore has it are all descended from thirty-six families from Dawei, originally invited to live here by two brothers, who had come to the area and impressed the Nyaungshwe *sawbwa* with their hard work. The fishermen's rowing technique is famous. They stand in their boats, with their outer legs wrapped around the oar, propelling it along. They row in this strange way because it allows them to see and avoid the water hyacinth and floating islands. Every so often they stop and pick up a huge upside-down cone-shaped wood-and-bamboo net to check for fish.

At the Nampan market, silver jewellery, lacquerware and silk lungis are in abundance.

'You look lady sisser, no problem.'

The Pa-O women are the most easily distinguish-able people by their black dresses and red-and-orange headdresses – which look like towels wrapped around wet hair. On the floor are their wares, black disc-like sweets, jaggery, and a type of ginger cake that tastes of nothing.

The lake's main shrine is the Phaung Daw U, which outside has an enormous gilt barge headed by a dragon with eyes of cricket-sized red glass balls, and inside has five golden statues which bring good luck if you rub them. Unfortunately they have been touched so often that they now resemble Mr Blobbys or bowling pins rather than the Buddha.

We stop at a wooden monastery in the middle of the lake. This is the Jumping Cat Monastery. Inside various moggies are lying around sleeping on the floor. They are surrounded by monks and a few English travellers with disconsolate looks on their faces. It is soon clear why. Every few minutes, the monks shake a box of cat biscuits and a few of the cats wake up. The monk then holds up a loop and whacks the chosen cat under the chin until it is tired of looking up and jumps up through the loop, and even then it's not always rewarded with a biscuit. Watching this we soon feel sheepish and unhappy. If it weren't for the travellers, these cats wouldn't have to do this in the first place. We all slink away hoping the monks will let the poor cats lie. If only they could run away, but they can't because they're surrounded by water.

On to a silver factory and there, a great surprise –
a magnificent black cat and his wife who has just had
kittens. Right, this is it. If there are any dark ones, any
little black things like the parents, I'm taking one home.
The owner displays the kittens, but as with black-haired
parents who then produce redheads these two have had a
litter of gingers. Disappointment.

Inle Lake is rather crowded and as soon as I see Mel and
Maxine's faces amongst the crowds in the market, I know
it's time to move on.

In my dreams I am bewildered. I move from one moment
to the next like a newborn child, utterly unknowing,
completely at a loss. I should really be grateful. At least I'm
asleep to dream. But perhaps insomnia is more preferable
to these torments to the soul. On waking I move to Kalaw
in order to trek to some mountain villages and monasteries
and finally get off the tourist track. The exercise will do me
good and take me out of myself. Ah, the eternal search for
peace and calm.

I walk behind my silent guide, whose name is Bin Heep.
It is a pleasant, cool climb up through tiny, quiet villages,
avocado and cheroot fields, past enormous centuries-old
trees and one bullock lowing in the wind. The bullock is
harnessed up and carries a cart full of bamboo trunks. It
steps carefully in dried red earth tracks. Colour brightens
our day in the form of red sprays of flowers (Christmas
flowers), purple and yellow blossoms and huge wisteria
trees. Children see us and cry 'Hello, hello, hello' for

miles past us until their voices are baby echoes on the wind. Dragon-flies silently flit and zip up and around.

Our first stop is a monastery where we sit down to a lunch of watery soup, cake and mango. The guest book has comments and signatures with smiley faces: 'We left at 7.13 and arrived at 10.54. Wonderful such piece (*sic*) and a great feeling of detachment from life. A great place to find yourself. Will always have this place in my heart.' Or 'Now with cheroot in hand I can chill out.' Aargh, the hideous words of hippiedom.

Lovely as it is up here, it's quite odd too. Firstly the monks have just broken into a rousing chorus of 'Danny Boy'. And secondly another monk has just offered me a lift to my next destination in his four-wheel-drive Suzuki 4000, retail price $25,000.

After lunch we start trekking again. After a while I ask if there are any loos at the reservoir we're heading to. Bin Heep says no and we trudge on. He tells me to walk on. He walks off the path himself. So I walk on a bit and have a pee. Voices can be heard and of course round the corner come several Burmese folk, as well as Bin Heep, all of whom get a great view of my white moon bum.

The women giggle and walk on but Bin Heep chides me: 'Say "I need a piss" if you want to, don't go on the road.'

Oh, soooo inelegant. We continue trekking.

The walk is rather beautiful, through lush green pine forests and blue misty mountains with patchwork fields of tomatoes, cheroot and bananas. We eat yellow raspberries from the bushes along the path. For tea we stop at a mountaintop house with a garden of hollyhocks, pink roses, lilacs, sweet peas, interspersed with trails of shiny black ants, huge yellow butterflies and furry caterpillars. We carry on to tiny villages and another monastery.

After a while the conversation inadvertently turns to politics.

'Our government very strong, very powerful,' says Bin Heep apropos of the trees which also, he has noted, are big and strong.

'What do you think a government is for?'

'To hold guns and control the people.'

'Hmm. And what do you think the government should spend its money on?'

'Weapons.'

'What about education or health?'

He thinks. It has never occurred to him before.

'Do you mind if the generals make themselves rich as they spend that money on weapons?'

'This does not happen.'

'Do you like this government?'

'It is OK. We are used to it.'

'Is that any reason to accept it?'

'When people have other ideologies, bad things happen.'

'But here people aren't allowed any ideologies other than the government's. They go to jail if they try something else. There is corruption and prostitution with this government. These things exist in any system, but at least with democracy, people are free to choose how they are governed.'

He is silent.

'You don't prefer a democracy?'

He looks bewildered.

'Why are you telling us what to do? This is not your country.'

I can't exactly disagree. This reminds me of the British refusing to take off their shoes last century. I suddenly realise I have no idea what the criteria for getting involved in another country's politics are. There are plenty of human crises the world over that are completely ignored.

'No, but humans have a collective responsibility to help each other.'

'We do not need your help. I am fine. I am safe. I can walk home late at night.'

He looks triumphant as though he has heard street violence is the big bogeyman of Western countries.

'But so can I!'

'Really?'

'Really.'

I keep quiet about the Harrow Road being dodgier than ever, and that gentrification seems to be bypassing parts of W9.

'And what price your safety? Wouldn't you prefer free speech?'

'What is that?'

'When everyone is free to say what they want. Your

newspapers are controlled by the state. There are no free independent articles.'

I feel very middle class waxing and waning about democracy, feminism and liberalism. I might as well be at a dinner replete with Chianti and Nigella Lawson cooking.

'Are you sure?'

'I am sure. I am positive.'

He thinks and then says angrily, 'Change should come slowly.'

'How slowly do you want, Bin Heep? Is forty years slow enough for you?'

'What should I do?'

A good question, but of course I have no answer. Get some guns, organise resistance and be prepared to die in the fight for democracy? I don't think so.

Next, a village, where the people make their money from tea. Seven families live together in a long house. Along the length of the house are seven cubicles where the parents sleep and couple privately – so to speak. Parents have their children marry at about thirteen or fourteen so that the children stay in their villages. However, they know very little about sex so they don't get started on that until later. The children are filthy dirty, covered in rags and snot. The women do all the work, pick the tea, dry it, choose the best leaves, while the men sit around smoking and chatting and gambling all the money away. Bin Heep senses that this annoys me, and tells me slowly and carefully several times that the men organise the family.

'Can't the men chat for just a couple of hours and help with the work the rest of the time?'

'Maybe. The women work hard but they are happy.'

'I'd like to talk with them. Will you ask them what they hope for in their lives?'

'They don't know.'

'How do you know without asking them?'

'They don't know any better.'

'But they've seen cars in town and food and clothes in the market — do they want those?'

(There seems nowhere else for my head to go — either noble savage or corrupt capitalist. Is there no other way of living? Is there nothing in between?)

'Haven't the women thought of spreading the work more evenly? Could you ask them for me?'

'No.'

'Why not?'

'Because they might not let me come again with other tourists.'

'Perhaps they're not that fascist, Bin Heep. Perhaps they can take a balanced view knowing that one comment does not change the world. And will they assume all tourists have the same opinion?'

'They're uneducated and very simple.'

'Yes, and they'll stay that way with you around. Your thinking reflects that of your government.'

'The tourists, they walk in, quick look, and then go. They ask nothing. You ask too many questions.'

'Will you ask them if they want to know anything about my life?'

He is silent.

'Bin Heep, please?'

He translates, and two of the women ask a couple of things. Bin Heep is silent.

'What do they say, Bin Heep?'

'They want to know where you're from.'

'London, England.'

I smile at them.

They look puzzled and look at Bin Heep. His reply is rather longer than just 'London, England' and I get the feeling that they asked something else which he didn't feel like translating. They have the same feeling too, and soon we are talking at Bin Heep.

'Tell me the truth, Bin Heep. What did they really ask?'

They are slightly irritated too, asking things repeatedly, and tapping him and waving towards me as if to say 'Go on! Ask her!' But Bin Heep will not play ball. It is frustrating.

As we walk away, he says, 'They are simple people. They don't want to know about your ways.'

'That's not how it seemed to me.'

'You are exceptional lady.'

He smiles, but his smile is that of a crocodile – teeth only, eyes black and frowning.

Back at the Viewpoint Lodge, where we are to spend the

night, another traveller has turned up with his trekking guide. Bottle tops have been arranged in a smiley 'welcome' sign on the ground. I asked Bin Heep specifically not to take me on a tourist trail. Geesh! The other traveller, Fritz, is a Teutonic Jeremy Beadle. His eyes are sunken, his hair is a mane of curly mouse, his white caps have a thick line of black at the top and his skeletal grin shines out from wet pink gums. He turns out to be The World's Most Annoying German. He laughs about absolutely everything regardless of whether it's funny, which invariably it's not, and is accompanied by a similarly smile-all Burmese dude-like guide, name of Chaw Chaw, who even thinks his comment 'Beautiful sunset', or 'Shall we eat now?' hilariously funny.

So I am sitting in a bamboo hut on top of a mountain with some asinine people, supposedly having a great time. Needless to say, Sour Puss in the corner is keeping to herself, watching the owners cook over their open earth fire, inside their house. They sleep on rolled-up mats on a low platform on the other side of the room, and spend their days working the extremely steep hill fields.

Every time the other traveller says something like, 'Vee vant the Internet up here, yah,' I want to growl, 'Oh do us all a favour, Fritz, and shut it.' Finally I can bear it no longer, and feel sorry for the guides who are drunk, bored with plumbing the depths of their past tense and subjunctive-free English, and desperate for a gossip in Burmese.

So I huff off in the direction of one of the huts, having

first washed scrappily from a bucket of water the dogs had been drinking from.

Out there in the dark, Bin Heep moves towards me.

'Do you feel unsafe?' he asks menacingly. 'Do you want to sleep with the other traveller?'

'*What?* Sleep with Fritz? You have to be *kidding*.'

But I might as well be sleeping with him because there is a gap at the top of one of the walls, and later I hear Fritz undressing and snuffling down. I hear every stomach rumble, every fart and cough he emits that night.

Ahhh. To be on a mountain, having walked all day, and eaten well (er, sort of) ready for a good night's sleep.

Tum ti tum.

Oh Christmas night, not again.

Now insomnia is something I know about. Semiotics, no. The whys and wherefores of fly-fishing. No. What the hell the prawn-peeler inventor was thinking of. No. But insomnia, yes.

Though of course no one knows as much as my Chilean ex boyfriend Pablo. He once woke me up in the middle of the night with a harsh bedside light and a request for entertainment. I turned over and told him to tell himself a story. Which he did out loud and it went like this (it was all in Spanish but I think I got the gist):

'There was once a beautiful prince who lived with a beautiful princess. When one night the prince couldn't sleep and asked the princess to help him she selfishly turned over and went back to sleep. So he felt no guilt whatsoever when he tore both her arms out of her sockets and beat her over the head with them till she was dead, then gnawed the flesh off them like they were engorged chicken wings and spat the bones out, which made a *ptui* noise as they tinkled on the floor.'

I stared in horror at him but then waylaid my own early death by pointing out that the bones would only make a *ptui* noise on the floor if they were dry, which by the sound of things they couldn't possibly have been, but he was staring maniacally at me by this stage so I simmered down.

An hour later I was woken by the sound of my own piano gustily belching forth Led Zeppelin, or was it Scott Joplin? Whatever, it was weird in the blackness of the night. I felt I was suddenly in a ghost-town cowboy saloon, with a pianola playing by itself. I switched on the sitting-room lights, and there was Liberace at the piano, able to play without lights and/or indeed the permission of those trying to sleep nearby.

After arranging for Pablo to spend an enjoyable four weeks at St Thomas's Looney Bin in Tooting, I was able to continue my life.

Ah, Claudius. The pain of losing him is now a desensitised shadow sleeping in the spare room. But I don't feel sorted. I don't really know where I'm going. Is my search for cats the best way to live in the present? Does it give my life meaning? I'm trying to find meaning. And yet I'm getting nowhere. But if you don't play ball in life, if you don't go for it with a sincere 'Go, girrrrl' rugby-tackle attitude, you're really stuffed. But the moments of lucidity or fatigue, when you realise every effort leads to the constant whirr of the hamster's wheel, rather than fulfilment, or happiness, or whatever it is that will give a moment's peace, can be, well, deflating.

TEN

KALAW TO BAGO (SORT OF) TO RANGOON TO BANGKOK TO LONDON

THE DEMONS OF last night seem to have receded for the moment. They are in the corner of the hut squabbling over who is going to wear my silk lungi, leaving me just the filthy trousers and shirt. As we trek on, Bin Heep tells me that people are afraid of cats. He hates them. Well, that pretty much sums him up. He and his wife had one yellow cat that left the house and a week later his son died. Recently another of their cats gave birth and brought the kittens into their bed to keep warm. In the night his wife rolled over and killed one by mistake, so he has to watch out in case any bad luck befalls him over the next few weeks. He says cats can predict the future. He doesn't say how, but I'm happy to believe him. Then inevitably we move back towards amateur politics.

'Bin Heep, what do you think of the universities being closed?'

'Good thing.'

'Why?'

'Because the students are noisy and disruptive and it is

best to control them by separating them. It's good for them to go to foreign universities.'

'You don't think that means the country loses its best pupils to other countries? And that means that only the rich can send their children to university. Do you think that's right?'

He thinks and then, 'Yes.'

'Why? Are you mad?'

It is only 8 a.m. on Day Two of our trek.

'What about the death penalty, Bin Heep? What do you think of that?'

'It is a good things.'

I fall silent but after a few minutes, Bin Heep speaks again.

'*No!* You must talk with me. You must talk with me.'

'Bin Heep, I am tired, and frustrated, talking to you.'

He stands in front of me and holds me tight by the arms till I want to squeal with pain.

'You will talk with me. You will carry on and shut up only when I tell you to.'

He looks me in the eye. There is something glinting in him as though he might, I don't know, lick me? Something perverse and strange. Not a thump across the face but something unexpected and nasty.

'Bin Heep, have you forgotten that I am employing you to take me on an interesting trek?'

'I have not forgotten. And you have not forgotten that you will pay me.'

'Get your hands off my arms this very *instant*.'

My throat growls with anger and my face shakes.

We arrive at a richer village than yesterday's. Here the youngsters decide who they want to marry. The people live in bamboo houses, not long houses, make baskets from bamboo and dress like the Pa-O. In fact this village seems so rich it brings to mind stories of girls who prostitute themselves in Thailand and send their money back to their families.

Next day, we get up very early while the stars and moon are still out. We walk for miles and miles to visit a family in Taungyo with two little ginger kittens. The little boy is very rough with them. He throws them around and batters them. I feed the kittens peanuts which they love and one kitten falls asleep exhausted on my lap. When I move, it feigns sleep as long as it can until I put it down. Poor little thing, being messed with day in and day out. It's the fluffiest, gingerest little thing.

The little boy makes the kittens' parents sit up like dogs and whacks them when they put their paws down. He pulls them by the tail. I ask him to be gentle. His father asks me questions. But Bin Heep answers for me and won't translate. The man then asks several questions about England, which Bin Heep answers without consulting me. I'm intrigued to know his answers, considering he's never been there.

Each time we visit a village, Fritz and Chaw Chaw are just ahead of us or behind us. I ask Bin Heep to find out which way they're going so that we can avoid them, but each time Bin Heep replies, 'Yes, yes,' and does nothing. Eventually we arrive at a train station. A man sells crabs from Rangoon, a woman wanders around with bunches of vibrant red-and-pink flowers with yellow centres. At a table by the tracks, under the sun, we eat a chicken curry with rice and boiled eggs.

Then we head off into the hills. After a while I see Fritz and Chaw Chaw just ahead. I stop.

'I really don't want to go on the same old tourist trail everyone does.'

'Yes, yes.'

'Bin Heep?'

'Yes?'

'Could you ask them which route they're taking and then take me on another?'

'But you don't want to walk with them.'

'Precisely. But as you speak Burmese you could talk to Chaw Chaw and find out . . . oh forget it.'

Bin Heep smiles.

So frustrating. I realise there's no point making such a fuss about this – I'm clearly on the same old route everyone else has done, and there's no way of avoiding it, certainly not with Bin Heep as my guide. And yet I can't help it. I am so frustrated by his attitude. And so tired from stinking of sweat and having blisters for three days.

'OK, Bin Heep, you win. Let's move on.'

'Fine.'

He moves on at a terrific pace, with my water bottle. After a few minutes he is way ahead of me and I can't keep up because of my blisters. I stay on the path but after a while I come to a crossroads. I have no idea which way to go. I have no sense of direction in the middle of Trafalgar Square, let alone the hills and lands around Kalaw. I shout Bin Heep's name. I shout again. No reply. I shout 'Heep, Heep, Heep' like a maniacal tweety bird but still no reply.

Soon I'm incredibly thirsty. All sorts of murderous thoughts flit through my head, but finally I just slump down under a tree and wait. I'm panicky and scared I'll never make it back to town. I'm in the middle of nowhere. I try to return to the railway station, but when I look in that direction all I see is a mass of hills.

About an hour later he shouts back. When he eventually shows up, I want to thump him, but instead I burst into tears. He laughs. I storm on, silent and angry, not really noticing the intense lush greenery of the surrounds, the close hills and the red earth. But finally I can't be bothered to be angry, and we're at peace.

Near the end, like a child, I ask Bin Heep how long until we are home. Ah. Home sweet home. If only it really were home. He says 'Fifteen minutes' about six times. I am utterly exhausted. New blisters pop up on my feet like the bubbles in overcooked porridge. The first human I see is a woman piling manure into her car. She offers me a lift. We drive for a good while until we're back at the guest house. I always fantasise about being a hiker. Oooh let's hike here and trek there, trekky trekky trek trek, but actually I hate it.

This guest house is a dump. The lino on the floor has great ruts, the towels are dirty and the walls are so thin (being made of any old ramshackle bits of cardboard nailed together randomly) that I can hear the family in the next house clearer than my own thoughts.

I take my first shower in three days, in the communal showers, but ooh the black damp patches on those bathroom walls are something else. I stand under that shower holding every bit of me in so as not to touch the walls and the moths and flying things around me. The spaces above and below the walls allow any passer-by to hear what I'm doing – arrrgh, heeby-jeeby time.

Back in my room, my filthy towel stinks. I drip dry, unwilling to touch anything, frozen in the middle of the room, like a shop mannequin. And there's a little white worm wriggling on my clothes. It is difficult to work out where the bodyless voices all around me are coming from. Under my bed perhaps? I feel rather quiet and introverted. Still, I have tonight to look forward to. The woman who gave me the lift invited me to supper at her house.

When she arrives, I jump up and get my things. I'm dismayed, on closing my door, having pressed the lock button on the inside, to find in my hand not my keys as I'd thought but my toothpaste.

She lives in a large colonial house, surrounded by jasmine and jacaranda trees, which is home to a destitute family and several adopted children, thanks to her generosity. She is very religious, saying often, 'I believe in Gout.' She is generous, warm and kind, her food is delicious, and I wish I could lay my head on her bosom and cry for two hours, cry about her country, cry about my fatigue, cry about my failed project. I want to feel as though I'm on the earth rather than on stilts.

'Perhaps you need to stop and rest,' she says, her hand on my shoulder, sensing the state I'm in. 'Why don't you go to Kyaiktiyo?'

'What is it?'

'A pilgrimage site, where an enormous golden boulder sits precariously at the top of a mountain. It's very beautiful.'

'Have you seen it?'

'Oh no. We're not allowed to travel.'

'Isn't it ironic that a stranger sees more of your country than you do?'

'It is sad. But this is our reality.'

Waiting at the bus station in Kalaw for a fourteen-hour bus ride that stops at Bago at 4 a.m., before continuing to Rangoon, I admire the hand-drawn posters for that famous film, *Point Blink*. From Bago I can go to Kyaiktiyo on another eight-hour bus ride.

Bin Heep walks in – well, it's a small town. We say polite hellos. I can't be bothered to hike my way through the virgin jungle of his English.

Almost the second I'm on that bus I regret it. Why didn't I take a plane? So what if the money goes to the government? Perhaps that's why people shouldn't come here: because the exhaustion of Southeast Asia brings out the survival instinct – and that instinct is enough to kill others, if the money paid for comfort lines the pockets of the oppressors.

Meanwhile the guy next to me discreetly spits betel into a bag – unfortunately it's plastic so I can see its slimy red mauled contents. He keeps trying to touch me, so I nudge him away. He asks where I'm getting off and I say Bago. Then his unwashed little boy keeps trying to spread out on to my lap. I'm in an agony of squashed discomfort for the majority of the journey. We wind down the mountains for two hours in boiling heat while the coach's TV blasts a terrible Burmese film. The air-conditioner is rarely on. Then at night when it is cooler, it blasts away at morgue speed.

My inability to sleep on anything moving means that I sleep between 9 p.m. and 10 p.m. and 3.30 a.m. and 4.30 a.m. I'm aware of movement at some stage and the guy next to me gets off. He looks very shifty, but I turn over and doze on. When I wake up properly I realise we have already passed through Bago and that my neighbour was getting off there too but didn't tell me. I fight my way to the front of the bus and ask, 'Bago? Bago?' They don't understand. I then try my appalling Burmese on them, but not surprisingly this is even worse. The men stop the bus and drop my bag in the road. They point back along the way we came and drive off.

I'm in no-man's-land. It is pitch black, with not a street light or a house in sight. A car pulls up and the driver offers me a lift to Rangoon. I give him money to take me in the

opposite direction to Bago. He drives away. I storm off
with my backpack on my back, making quiet whiffling
noises. As I tramp along this silent blackened road I'm
angry and fed up.

Why am I putting myself through this? There are no
Burmese cats in Burma. There's an ugly political regime
that's made me so lonely I've taken to imagining my dead
cat is still here. Why go and visit this rock in Kyaiktiyo?
Why endure another fruitless pilgrimage when what I really
need has to come from me? The point about a country like
this is that you can't be independent unless you speak the
language. If you don't, you're dependent *for everything* on
everyone around. What I really need is me – is home. I'm
going home.

At this moment a bike rides by. It's going in the wrong
direction, away from Rangoon, but it's transport, and I
realise I have to take what's on offer. I must go away
from Rangoon in order to get to Rangoon. Yes, it's all
very deep. It is fiendishly uncomfortable on the back of
that bike, but half an hour later we arrive in Bago. The
second I'm off the bike I start negotiating a lift to Rangoon.
I'm going to the airport and getting out of this depressing
country. I'm going home. Finally I find a car bound for the
city. After an hour we start but then stop in every town –
about five times – for five minutes, even though no one
seems even slightly keen to go to Rangoon. An exercise
in patience that I fail miserably.

When we reach Rangoon, I've no idea where they'll
drop me. But we end up at the bus station. The other

passengers shout to the vulture taxi drivers, and point at me. The taxi drivers don't understand 'Airport', but they do understand 'Air Force'.

Once at the airport, I wash my hands and face and have fried rice, an egg and a pot of tea for breakfast. All the clocks say something different so I almost miss my flight. I give all my kyat away to the loo cleaners. One points to her teeth, or rather the gaps between her teeth – I think the money's going towards some dentistry.

Back in recognisable territory, other passengers, mainly German women all with the same hair colour, a vibrant tart red, but different hairstyles, a sixties bob or a twenties bob or skinhead with feather fringes, giggle, take their last pictures, unwrap their lacquerware souvenirs, like normal travellers who have had a good time. I don't think I'll crack a smile until I'm back in my flat.

Finally I'm in Bangkok. I soon realise though that my problems have only just begun. Unfortunately, because I do not have my aeroplane ticket, thanks to the thief from the monastery, the airline is unwilling to change my flight. And because I don't have my credit card either it is impossible to get myself a new ticket back to London. Trying to change my original flight means lugging my bag all over the airport, from office to office, which makes my back twitch moodily. Advised to call the central office in town, I then change money, buy a phone card, work out the codes, call other airlines, BA, Air France and Thai Air, which has a million different ticket offices. Back and forth from the third floor to the second to Terminal 1 to Terminal 2 back to . . . hell.

Then I decide that if I can't get a ticket to London I might as well go to Phuket and lie on a beach, but this involves going on standby and returning to the booth every half an hour. It's not that good an idea anyway considering I'm running short on cash (and no one will accept a $100 bill that is legal tender, but has a smaller design on it than the more recent ones). By this stage I'm exhausted and phone a friend in London and burst into tears. The Thai girls in the phone office laugh at my childish display of emotion. But my friend organises a flight home for me, so I relax.

I take my sleeping pill thirty minutes before take-off, not expecting the plane to be delayed, which of course it is, so I'm slumped like a tramp over my bag and falling over the next chair for a while until some worried passengers kindly weave me on to the plane.

At last I feel the cool air of London on my face, after flying low over the neat suburban houses with their plots of garden. Everything is clean and quiet, no cars honking at all hours. Back in my flat, I relish the soft carpet under my feet after all those bare dirty floors. I scrub and soak for hours in the bath. I sit on my sofa in the silence. And smile.

Never again will I complain about anything to do with this country, this government, and for the time being anyway, this weather. The escalators at Notting Hill Gate tube station may never work, but essentially everything else does. I can go anywhere I like, and short of taking my clothes off in public, do anything and say anything I want without getting arrested. I can demonstrate in Trafalgar Square for cats to be compulsory pets, I can launch a newspaper that only publishes articles on seaweed, I can pogo-stick to the ends of the earth if I feel like it. I've never appreciated this before, always taken it for granted, never so viscerally understood the full meaning of the words: we are free. And so I jig a little dance of freedom around my flat until I wrick my ankle on the step between the kitchen and living room and explete throatily. Calming down after the last oath has popped out of my Tourette's syndromed mouth, I am engulfed by the silence once more. Ah.

After a second it's a bit too silent. In the old days when I returned from trips, Claudius would be at the top of the stairs to greet me, and his pretend sulks and reproachful chit-chat for having left him would soon be whisked away with cuddles and presents of exotic food. Soon we'd both be lying on the sofa, so close his whiskers would tickle my nose and his purrs deafen my ears. Now the place feels empty and ghostly. Hmm. My mission to find another perfect cat has not been what you'd call entirely successful. Actually it's been a complete disaster. Well, no surprise in Burma – and no matter. There's still Thailand.

PART THREE
THAILAND

ELEVEN

LONDON TO BANGKOK

IN THAILAND THE rainy season has started, and, not wanting a permanent Thingyan experience, I decide only to continue my search for the perfect cat once it has stopped raining. So I have a few free months in London. After I've come down from the high of getting back I am slightly ashamed of having found Burma so difficult. I don't know whether my anger has been due to Burma's situation, Southeast Asia in general, or just me. I suspect all three. Ironically, in England I am now much more aware of a lack of family community, an abundance of me-me-me-ness and general isolation. Of course I'm more than guilty of 'That's enough about me. What do you think about me?' – but I take it as a by-product of this powerful freedom which allows us the luxury of aiming for personal fulfilment (in the form of cats or otherwise).

Hanging out with friends one night, I find myself at a restaurant next to a tall, lean, blond man.

'So you've been to Burma?' he says. 'I've always wanted to go there.'

'Well, don't,' I reply. 'Even if you're really careful, most

of your money ends up in the hands of the government.
I don't recommend it.'

'What did you think of it?'

'Depressing. Debilitating.'

'But isn't it beautiful?'

'Um, Bagan is pretty, and the Shwedagon is very shiny,
but I didn't find it outstanding, actually.'

'But it's very unspoilt, isn't it?'

'On the contrary – it is *completely* spoilt. There's no
McDonald's or Coke ads, and the people wear lungis, but
they're really poor, their country's resources are plundered
by neighbouring nations and they have no real freedom.'

'So why did you go?'

'To look for a Burmese cat,' I reply, feeling sheepish.

'I've always thought I'd make my fortune through cats,'
he says, undaunted.

'Really?' I perk up. 'How?'

'By attaching a tiny camera to my sister's cat and filming
its day-to-day activities (scrapping with the neighbour's cat,
hanging on to the scruff of its favourite female, having a
midnight snack) and then broadcasting it on the web.'

'I'm sorry? You'll make millions by –?'

'. . . *Billions*, not millions.'

I am tickled pink by this idea. The longer I talk to
him the more I feel that here is someone who might not
limit me. Other people try talking to us, but after a few
moments we naturally veer towards each other again. At
the end of the evening we say goodbye. He asks for my
number. I go home, my head full of him. I am really keen.

This happens very rarely. And the last time I felt this it led to disaster.

I was so relieved to be feeling something that I ignored signs this guy left me, like droppings, that he was an utter, well, dropping. Imagine being serious about a guy who:

i)   tells you the only position his ex-girlfriend (whom you know) could achieve orgasm in;

ii) pulls the tail of his very skinny Siamese cat saying, 'Treat her badly – like women. That's what they like';

iii) calls obsessively six times a day to tell you he loves you after only a week.

I just lapped it all up rather than thinking: Nutter alert. *Run!* Then one day I didn't hear from him again.

So as I muse on my interest in Cat Cam Man, I make a pact with myself to be open to all signs, to listen to his words and watch his actions and see exactly who he is, rather than only see what I want to see. Except he doesn't call. For ages. Finally he does and one date (dinner at a local restaurant) leads to another (a very obscure art-house film) and another (the Holocaust Exhibition at the Imperial War Museum. *Hello?*). He is still stimulating and funny. Not once does he show any signs of nutterdom. He is blissful. He becomes my official boyfriend.

After a while I feel a nagging. The rainy season is almost over. (In Thailand, I mean. In England it's never over.) It is time to be heading back East, and learning to travel without losing my temper. I am in the middle of something that I haven't finished. I am on a mammoth search for a cat.

Many people think that women who love cats are using them as relationship substitutes. I like to think that women who love cats – just love cats. (Of course there are advantages to living with someone who never answers back. But on the other hand you can only do so much with a being the height of your shin.) But I can't deny that the original reason for wanting *my* cat was to find an outlet for my love. Yet here in front of me is a lovable man.

There are two problems here:

i) I have a nasty feeling I have become one of those women who, having found love, is about to ditch all personal goals and ambitions: cat-owning in my case, similar to ignoring your friends because you have a new boyfriend. In short, a really stupid, un-independent thing to do.

ii) Who says this is love? How do I know? I thought it was last time and look what happened.

iii) (Actually there are three.) I still want a cat. Argh. What does it all mean? Am I just a chicken with humans and a lion with cats? Or a mother hen with cats and a tiger to men? I have to find out – what on earth I am talking about, if nothing else.

Preliminary research shows that looking for pedigree cats in Thailand is a perfectly sensible thing to do: there are catteries, there is no military dictatorship, there are extensive transport networks. I tell Cat Cam Man my plan. We say goodbye. I feel yearning – but I squelch it and move on, determined.

At first sight Bangkok seems a vast network of motorways, spewing out filth, smoke and choke – more Houston than a city of Eastern mystique. It seems to be hiding behind the rotating black blades of an aeroplane, so dark and alive is its pollution. Yet there's something exciting too. The vast skyscrapers, the unashamed adoption of Western eateries (McDonald's, Dairy Queen) and clothes (Gucci, Prada) exist alongside saffron-robed, barefoot monks with alms bowls wandering the streets, plastic makeshift roadside restaurants selling spicy noodle dishes, tiny shrines bedecked with jasmine garlands, sticks of incense, cigarettes and cakes. It is a country that has never been colonised. The city says yes to the invaders, gives them what they want, but takes plenty in return.

I wander the streets of Bangkok. Stalls sell bright phosphorescent yellow, red and pink sweets, rice wrapped in banana leaves, bits of meat on sticks, chopped pineapple, green mango, lengths of papaya, watermelon, boiled eggs, dumplings, bright-green and pink puddings in milk and bowls of juicy burgundy pomegranate seeds heaped on ice. Thais tend to graze rather than eat three square meals a day, hence the incredible quantities of food constantly available.

It's not clear what some shops are selling: two old men sit on a brown leather sofa in an empty, dingy room opened on to the street, with broken boxes piled in one corner. Other shops are packed with Chinese lanterns and colourful plastic boxes. The excess of things to eat, drink, smoke and buy is, miraculously, putting me off shopping.

The silly relief at 6 p.m. when you find a hotel room and realise you won't spend the night on the streets after all. Then after a while your eyes adjust to the room, and what looked like a large clean simple room in fact backs on to not one, not two, but three karaoke bars. The shower spurts water on to the walls, the ceiling, even the towel hanging carefully on the door two metres away, everywhere in fact but on you (except for a very fine dribble like that of an old sleeping man). The sink has a pipe that drops water an inch above your feet, soaking your shoes with your own salivaed toothpaste. And the caterwauling. I've never heard more sounds of humanity, from loo-flushing to burping, to hacking coughs, to sex, to singing, to shouting.

So it's best to be outside. The skytrain affords a bird's-eye view of the city without you having to encounter horrendous traffic or the depressing darkness of streets covered by flyovers. This bird's-eye view of the city reveals pockets of palm trees and woods hiding old wooden houses, smaller wooden shacks with corrugated-iron roofs and skyscrapers. Some buildings are green-mirrored wonders, but in amongst the very old and very new are hideous tenements, building sites, dirty old petrol stations, low-slung electricity wires, uneven pavements dotted with food stalls and ponds of stale, swampy-green sludge water.

Looking out I wonder whether the city still earns its official name: 'Krungthepmahanakhonamornratanakos-inmahintarayutthayamahadilokpopnoparatanarajthaniburir-omudomrajniwesmahasatarnamornpimarnavatarsatitsakatti-yavisanukamprasit', which means 'City of angels, great city of immortals, magnificent jewelled city of the god Indra, seat of the King of Ayutthaya, city of gleaming temples, city of the King's most excellent palace and dominions, home of Vishnu and all the gods'.

Bangkok, the shorter version, comes from *Bang* (river-side village) and *makok* (plum), from before the city was made a capital in 1782. Although perhaps they could take a syllable or two from the longer version to form a new, more appropriate-sounding name: Mudom or Popnop.

My hotel is by a motorway. My room is behind a huge neon-lit advertisement which brightens and then fades throughout the night. I feel like an eye blinking. My first night I am woken by a cat yowling outside. By morning the cat is still yowling. I breakfast overlooking the choked, standstill traffic. Next door is one of Bangkok's ubiquitous Internet shops, packed with boys machine-gunning chickens in horridly violent video games. The screams they let out – the boys, not the chickens – are blood-curdling.

I have no desire to linger here so I phone Martin Clutterbuck, Bangkok's resident Siamese-cat expert, who translated the ancient Thai cat poems in his book *The*

Legend of Siamese Cats. He tells me to take the Chao Phraya express to Thon Buri and he'll meet me there. The Chao Phraya, the river running through Bangkok, is lined with expensive hotels with white, fairy-lit trees.

Getting on the boat is something else. It bangs untethered against the pier while passengers jump off and on – hoping they won't slip into the filthy brown water churning angrily below. Just as you are about to step on, the boat heaves away leaving a greeny brown swirl of water ready to engulf you. The boy with the rope does much whistle-blowing, guiding the driver closer to the dock, and then people spring off the boat and others pounce on.

Martin meets me off the boat and we drive to his home on a motorbike. Bumping over pot-holes, he competes with buses for tiny spaces, and I find myself clamping my legs inwards so that they won't be knocked off. His house has a large garden in which his traditional applehead Siamese cat roams. It is a lovely chunky thing, but is docile as a dormouse.

'The Siamese character is good evidence that the cats have evolved along with humans,' he says, as the cat allows us to cuddle and play with it any which way. It's the type of cat you could dress up in baby clothes and give a dummy to. Seeing him with his cat makes me miss Claudius, whose way of pressing his body against mine when he was settling down to sleep was a vote of entitlement that always managed to shove me off the bed.

'I've been told lots of different stories about the Siamese cat. Do you know its origins?'

'There are several different histories over here,' he replies. 'One has it that the King of Siam was given a very rare white cat, which he bred with the darker-furred sacred temple cats. Another cross-breeding story is that about three hundred years ago Annamese cats were crossed with the Sacred Cat of Burma. This took place after the victory of the Siamese and Annamese people over the Cambodian empire of the Khmers. Yet another story is that the local cats of Siam mutated so that their all-over dark-brown coat became temperature-dependent.'

'Became what?'

'Temperature-dependent. It's one of the breed's many extraordinary characteristics. When they are first born, hot from the womb, they are creamy-white all over. When they cool down their extremities get darker. If a limb is bandaged for a long time, the limb is lighter when uncovered, due to the heat.'

'I didn't know that. And have you always loved cats?'

'I suppose so. Actually I only got a cat as a mouser,' says Martin. 'One cat I got from Chatuchak market was half wild and drugged, because when it woke up it ran away. The market used to be an endangered-species supermarket, where tourists bought baby gibbons and then had no idea what to do with them. Luckily since then there's been a clamp-down but cats and dogs are still available.'

His large raggedy smile of varying shades of ivory lights up when his Thai wife, with a pendant of Rama V (King Chulalongkorn) around her neck, brings beer and crisps. She is very shy and doesn't look me in the eye.

'Ahh, this is the life,' he grins. 'Beautiful weather, cheap living. You can't get this in London. I also love the way the plants grow here. You have to scythe things back, they spring up almost over night. Every morning we're woken up by a cacophony of bird song.'

Martin gives me the names and addresses of various catteries throughout Thailand and hands me a leaflet about the forthcoming Bangkok Cat Show at the Rama Gardens Hotel.

First on his list is the Arirat Cattery. It is on the outskirts of Bangkok where the motorways finally become double roads, then single roads, then back roads, then lanes, then alleys. I walk beside waterways lined with shacks. Finally I spy cages containing the strangest cats I've ever seen: white with one blue and one green eye.

'Which cats are these?' I ask the approaching owner, Mr Aree.

'Khaomanee,' his daughter Arirat replies.

She explains that the Thais like this breed because they look nice and clean.

I spy a back cage with a fleabitten black cat with no tail.

'Oh, it's Japanese!' says Arirat. 'Very precious!'

Right.

Their favourite cats run free inside the house, which is jammed with trophies from cat shows. A champion Khaomanee jumps between them, scratching her whiskers against them as if to say 'Look what I won! ME!'.

'Who are you?' she purrs.

'A visitor from London, looking for a cat,' I reply in Cat, picking up a pretty female brown Burmese and scratching her under the chin.

'But you already have a cat,' she smiles.

'What do you mean?'

My mind is only half on her because I can feel the Burmese's muscles tense as she springs off my lap and scuttles to the other side of the room. She doesn't like my scratching technique.

'That brown cat by your feet.'

I look down and see nothing.

Just then Arirat offers me a bright-red drink that tastes like medicine.

'Which other cats do the Thais like?'

'Ginger, like tiger, and three-coloured because lucky,' she replies.

Just then a beautiful female Burmese, only six months old, walks in. Mr Aree's eyes light up.

'Eight thousand baht!' he smiles.

'Tell me,' playing for time, as I want to tot up mentally how much that is, 'your Siamese outside has a kink in her tail. Why do the Siamese cats have kinks?'

Mr Aree looks dumbstruck, so Arirat takes over.

'The kink was the result of a princess slipping her rings on to her favourite cat's tail when bathing in the river. She was called back urgently by the king and she left the cat behind, who slept the night with his tail under his paw so as to prevent the rings falling off. By morning he had a permanent kink.'

'Oh fascinating,' I smile, concluding £130 or thereabouts.

'Too early,' I continue, pointing at the Burmese girl. 'Journey only just begun. Need to see other cats. Where else can I find cats?'

'Tempoo.'

'I'm sorry?'

'Tempoo. Wat.'

'Temples? *Wats*?'

'*Krup*.' (Thai for yes.)

I take the express boat up the Chao Phraya river to the flower market at Thewet and the nearby Wat Nanarat where I believe there are cats galore. Cats traditionally were kept in *wats* to guard ancient texts from mice. Nowadays unwanted kittens are left at temples. Thewet flower market sells purple-and-white orchids, lotus, tiny yellow-and-pink roses, tight garlands of fuchsia, heavy jasmine ringlets (bought as offerings for temples) and other blooms such as the charmingly named 'Lady Who Wakes Late' because its petals open only at 10 a.m. and close in the late afternoon. The market also sells big and small turtles in buckets, sea eels, and huge shrimps. I buy a small basket of fish for the cats.

Supposedly guarding the temple wall and a drum sacred to Wat Nanarat are a large group of cats – all are moggies, some are tailless and one kitten has bleeding, bulging red eyes like a creature from *Star Wars*, a poor little thing that is scrawny and tiny. The scene is more horror film than cat nirvana. That poor kitten with the bulging bloody eyes comes to me and begs for a home. Another kitten, so young it is naturally blind, feels its way shakily, not knowing how to eat, not knowing how to drink. I put water on my fingertips and a piece of fish but the kitten needs milk. I want to drown it – it would be kinder. I want to cry.

Looking after them are two women, one of whom through incessant betel-chewing has now only black gaps with reddened brush sticking out like old bits of Shredded Wheat for teeth. She takes my fish, breaks it into pieces and mixes it in with rice. She then rips up pieces of newspaper as plates for the cats. The older ones have different approaches: a mottled brown–and–white cat is affectionate and waits patiently, knowing her turn will come, another is less philosophical and growls, hisses and scratches to get in there first. The other woman gives me a warm drink of sugary milk, which I try unsuccessfully to feed to the kittens.

I ask questions about the cats, my gestures increasing with each misunderstood sentence until I look deranged.

The two women talk to each other. They seem to be saying:

'She's barmy.'

'Yup, totally lost it.'

'Shame, she seems young.'

'Not that young. Look at the bags under her eyes.'

'Oh Rita! You are naughty . . .'

Or some such.

That evening I take in some Thai boxing at the Lumpinee Stadium. This sport was banned in the twenties because it was so dangerous (boxers used to bind their fists with bandage and glass-impregnanted kemp to damage their opponents) but was reintroduced in 1937 with rules banning biting and head-butting. I'm the only girl in the standing-room area, surrounded by Thais shouting 'Hee Hee' or 'Eek Eek' or 'Ding Ding' every time a boxer knees his opponent in the kidneys as they cling to each other's necks. The spectators, one arm in the air, flutter the fingers on that hand, like dancing girls in a revue. It must be some form of betting, though it is completely unclear how anyone is accountable. All I understand from the score cards is that all the boxers weigh less than me. Music plays while they fight, and at the end they bow elaborately, down on one knee, their arms stretched back, open and wide, in a sort of dance. They bow the *wai kru* to their trainers in respect. The boys wear amulets around their biceps for good luck.

Today another foray to another cattery on the outskirts. Full of hope, I'm met by a terrible stench: row upon row of dirty cages with cats in terrible condition, all

mewling piteously. There is one enormous Burmese stud
– the size of a sheep. But the other cats, some Burmese,
some Siamese, some plain moggy, are scrawny, mewing,
miserable and lonely. In one corner I spy a tiny black thing
with a cut above her eye and a cough. I ask how much
and the owner has the cheek to say 1,000 baht (about
sixteen quid).

'With the condition you keep your cats in, you should
pay me that just to take her away,' I mutter.

I point at a Siamese straight–tail.

'No kink?'

'No kink,' he replies. 'Do you know why they had
a kink?'

'Yes, because of the princess,' I reply confidently.

'Princess? There was no princess. There was a monk. A
monk who often left his pair of Siamese cats to guard his
golden goblet. He went away so often that one day his
male cat got fed up and went to look for another owner,
and while he was away the female stared at the goblet so
hard she gave herself a squint. She was so exhausted that
she wrapped her tail around the goblet and fell asleep.
When the male cat returned with a new monk, she had
given birth to a litter of kittens all with crossed eyes and
kinks in their tails.'

I prefer Arirat's story.

'You travel alone?' he continues.

'Er, yes, I do.'

'Ah well, you must take note of the story, young lady.
If you go away too often, you will lose your man!'

When he says this, I immediately think of Cat Cam Man, and then feel both guilty and excited as though I've just slipped Freudianly. His comment is somewhat uselessly patriarchal in this context, however, considering both the monk and the male cat were the ones to do the travelling. So I make my excuses and leave.

Back in Bangkok I stop for some reflective sightseeing at the Grand Palace, the former royal residence and home to King Chulalongkorn, lover of cats, hoping his spirit might guide me as to whether I should buy the little black girl or not. She's neither a boy, nor brown, nor Burmese, nor healthy. She is nothing I want and yet she is sweet. But once there I decide Buddha might be a better guide, so I go into the Wat Phra Kaeo, Bangkok's foremost temple, the resting place for the sacred Emerald Buddha. Discovered in 1434 in Chiang Rai by an abbot after lightning struck the *chedi* containing it, the image has been held in great esteem ever since. The *bot* containing it is impressive: the walls are decorated with murals of scenes from the Buddha's life, and the doors are intricately carved with mother-of-pearl detail, but the green image itself is tiny, sitting atop an enormous pedestal surrounded by umpteen golden Buddha images of varying sizes.

The hordes of tourists are barefoot and silent, all with their feet tucked under them. It is very rude to point your feet at anyone, particularly at the Buddha image, as the Thais believe the head is the highest point and most sacred part of the body and the feet the lowest. In fact, when addressing the king, whose feet are believed to be higher than mere mortals' eyes, the mere mortal refers to himself as 'under soles, coarse visible dust, fine invisible dust, gracious feet'. Some tourists bow three times in emulation of the Thais *wai*ing at the front. The *wai* in olden times was used to show that no weapons were in the hands.

Wandering around the forecourts, under a raging sun, I'm agog at the blast of colours – the gold of an enormous *chedi* (an upside-down bowl with a spire) housing a part of the Buddha's breastbone, the delicate reds, China-blues and greens of exterior porcelain, the multi-tiered red-and-green or blue-and-red tiled roofs with gilded *cho fas* (tassels of air) at the corners for protection, shaped like garudas, vicious, mythological things, half man, half bird. Dazzling. The place is awash with coloured glass, golden domes stretching to the sky and golden mosaics. I pause by Apsonsi, another mythical creature, half lion and half woman, wondering whether to get the cat or not.

This thought is momentarily interrupted by a school brass band playing 'Eye of the Tiger'. Surreal. After a brief absorption of the mother-of-pearl-inlaid doors, the sparkling gold Buddha and *bot* decorated with blue glass and mosaics, I step outside the temple complex. Just there is another black cat, the chunkiest, friendliest, purringest thing. I sit there with him, my heart lost again, wondering whether I should take *him* along with me instead.

The girls in the souvenir shops are tickled pink at the idea of an English girl coming all this way for a black cat, because 'They uhluhkee,' breathes one petite girl delicately. The girls crowd around me staring and there is much giggling behind hands. Now I need to think even more, the girl or this boy? I'm sneezing furiously. I've obviously developed an allergy since Claudius's death, either to heat or to the smell of dirty cages, or something.

Next day, giving cats a break, I take a tuk tuk to the famous Khao San Road, to look at the backpackers. And what a bunch of smelly hippies they are. And what a horrid overpriced road full of ugly things to buy and tasteless overpriced food it is. I hop in another tuk tuk. Tuk tuks, so named because of the engine noise, are covered motorbikes, with a bench seat at the back. Draped sometimes in Christmas lights, like a Santa ride, they are ridiculous and yet irresistible. You can see very little because of the low roof, and they are completely open to the elements. Being stuck behind a smoke-spewing bus is not even slightly amusing.

Before getting in, I agree on a price and the bargaining goes something like this:

'Chang?'

'Yes, get in.'

'How much?'

'Yes, get in.'

'No! How much?'

'Um Chang, velly velly far, so 200 baht.'

'Not on your nelly. It's round the corner and I paid 40 baht coming this way.'

'OK, 150 baht.'

'Don't be ridiculous! 40 baht.'

'OK, 150 baht,' motioning at me to get in.

I stand resolutely by the side of the road, looking for another tuk tuk. Sometimes this backfires horribly as the guy drives off, and I am left alone and transport-free, feeling a bit of a twit; sometimes it brings about a speedy agreement; sometimes we go through the following charade:

'OK, 140 baht.'

'No, 40.'

'OK, 130 baht. Lahs plice.'

'No, 40.'

'OK, 120 baht. Special flend plice.'

And so on.

But I'm OK this time. Except the journey doesn't seem quite long enough. I sense he's dropped me at the wrong place. I check where I am before paying (terribly clever, I think), find I'm right and then insist he takes me to the Chang boat stop. Annoyed at being caught out, he drives like the Evel Knievel of Bangkok tuk tuks. We screech around corners, honking at every other vehicle, through lights, in between buses, it's terrifying. As we approach an enormous roundabout my eyes widen and my ears slam back against my head. Sure enough as we head for the first curve too fast and not tight enough, the neighbouring Mercedes starts to turn, right into us. I have a choice: get scraped to death on the road or veer towards the terrifying oncoming Merc. I do the latter and lean in the opposite direction from the fall. In slow motion we overturn and slam the inner pavement with an ugly smell of dust, tarmac, spilling petrol and grit.

Only by my extraordinary acrobatic monkey-like cling-ing attitude do I manage to prevent the entire length of skin on my leg from being ripped off, as the driver's was, once his flimsy cotton trousers had given way first. The sight of blood (so red!) and his yelping and the honks of cars further back not knowing what's going on and the shouts of the guilty and terrified Mercedes driver, an angry businessman, and the heat overwhelm me. Covered in dirt and grime, my mouth full of dust, but miraculously unhurt apart from tears to clothing and bruising, I have an intense desire to be on a peaceful desert island by the sea.

Soon helping hands right the dented tuk tuk, and surrounding people laugh and slap me on the back. Hold on a minute, just how funny is this? Everyone discusses what happened. For a second I feel as if I'm in Italy. I hobble out of the road, shaken and stirred, and wait until an ambulance comes. But it doesn't. The guy gets into another tuk tuk. Bloody and bruised, he notices me and shouts, 'Hoh! 40 baht!'

I stare, incredulous.

'You want me to pay you for almost killing me?'

His driver laughs and speeds off.

And that's that. I'm too dazed to do anything other than accept a lift to Chang. Then the girl selling boat tickets tries to charge me 350 baht for an 8-baht boat ride. After a few angry words I'm finally on the boat. People stare.

I get off at the Oriental Hotel, hoping to be calmed by the peace and splendour of the white sofas, wooden chandeliers and huge bunches of lotus flowers, perhaps even treating myself to some ludicrously priced afternoon tea, but of course I'm turned away as I look like a tramp. I want to explain that I've been in an accident but am speechless, so find a taxi, get roundly ripped off because I'm too tired to argue, make it back to the hotel and retire to bed, sincerely hoping I'll never ever have to get out of it again.

After a while I wake up feeling very ill, my throat sore, my head achey. I gargle with some Dettol, which seems to be the equivalent of gargling with floor cleaner, because it burns all the hairs from my nostrils down to my tongue and I can't feel my neck any more. Should I have used TCP instead?

Next day, shaken and somewhat stirred, I take a boat to Nontaburi, which means 'Town of Happiness', in search of another cattery on Martin's list. A huge fat guy meets me off the boat and shows me the way.

'My name is Tiny!' he says, offering his hand and holding open the door of a taxi for me.

'But you're not tiny,' I can't help remarking, showing a complete lack of tact.

'No, this is my nickname. We all have them. They relate to our childhood, not to now – otherwise I would be called "Great Fat Pig", don't you think?'

He laughs very heartily and I titter and make uncovincing 'Oh absolutely not!' noises. The taxi potters down a maze of alleys and back streets while he explains more about names.

'Before 1913 Thais only had first names. In that year, King Vajiravudh, Rama VI, invented thousands of surnames because he loved the West so much. It was a great honour for a family to have one conferred on them.'

His cousin, the owner of the cattery, is a sweet girl and very friendly. She has cats in cages and cats running free in a room bare apart from wooden planks forming a ramshackle tree house. Out of the window there are two dogs fucking ferociously. The dog walks away, his penis a pink lipstick; the bitch looks both shell-shocked and bored. The cats are in good condition but none are right for me. There isn't that instant bond.

Another day, another dollar. In need of some good old-fashioned sightseeing, I hit Jim Thompson's house. Jim Thompson was responsible for bringing Thai silk to the world's attention. He was an architect but worked in Thailand as the head of the OSS (Office of Strategic Services). He was Mr Society in Bangkok and married a model – although the marriage split after six months. He disappeared in 1967 – like a cat going off to die alone – while walking in Malaysia. His disappearance has now notched up a few conspiracy theories, as the OSS was the forerunner of the CIA.

In the grounds of his peaceful house, I am accosted by a girl, another lone traveller, who raves about Thailand. Dodie looks Thai with jet-black locks and eyes to match – a mixture of Snow White and Cruella de Vil – but in fact has spent most of her life in Memphis and New

York. She is in Thailand finding long-lost roots.

'I lived in Bangkok with Mom for the first five years of my life. We lived in a haunted house where the ghost took a shower every evening and my mother couldn't sleep without Valium and whisky. We had to get in sixty monks to clear the place up.'

We bond a while before doing the tour and agree to spend the day together.

Jim Thompson made his house from six traditional teak houses which he brought from Ayutthaya – the capital of Thailand from the mid-fourteenth century until its sacking by the Burmese in 1767. Built on stilts, the house has wooden walls with ventilation slits at the top. The walls are held together by pegs, as the Thais believe that nails are for coffins. The house contains Venetian cherry cabinets, Irish Waterford crystal, colourful silk cushions and Chinese Ming vases. A high step at the entrance of each room keeps spirits out and babies in. Tables have claws for feet – three for a commoner, five for nobility and seven for royalty. On the walls are pictures of the Buddha giving away all his possessions, then his children and finally his wife.

'He get them all back in end, hap-py end-ing,' breathes our Thai guide in her evenly emphasised syllables.

'Oh look, he had a cat!' smiles Dodie meaningfully at me, while pointing at a Chinese porcelain cat-shaped chamberpot in one of the guest bedrooms.

We are joined by the usual bunch of tourists.

Says Dodie to the elephantine concubine to her left,

'Geez, it must be *hot* carrying all that extra weight around on ya!'

The woman looks distraught.

Meanwhile her Australian husband is saying to the guide, 'Jim Thompson must have been an interesting man. I bet he had lots of friends over, eh? I bet he showed them his nice things, eh? But it's strange he didn't take a Thai wife.'

He goes on for a while like this, until Dodie can take it no longer.

'He was *gay*! Duh!'

Her sonorous voice silences the room. Uplifted eyebrows meet her proud gaze.

'My father knew him,' she adds quietly, realising her comment needs back-up.

She looks down and then away modestly, perhaps to hide the fact that this is a blatant lie.

'Really?' I whisper as we stalk off, the falsely won respect of the rest of the room following her as she sails out of the room.

'Sure.'

'Your father knew him?'

'Hell no. Don't even know mah dad mahself. But come on. Of course he's a screamer. Beautiful pristine home, good with silks, designs, colour, and married to a model for six months? I just put two and two together.'

And got six.

After our tour we do some gentle shopping at Zen Central and the World Trade Center, enormous, air-conditioned shopping malls. Can Dodie shop. She shops with the ferocity and tenacity of a professional. And I can only admire that.

Finally we wander back out into the heat of the city. We are opposite the Erawan Shrine, named after Brahma's elephant Erawan, where people pray for good luck. It was erected to appease the land spirits, who were thought to be angry and therefore hindering the construction of the old Erawan Hotel – which in the fifties suffered one setback after another. The hotel then went up without a hitch. Stalls selling thick rings of jasmine and lotus wands (representing all living and growing things), or joss sticks and candles (symbolising fire and its purificatory qualities), line the street. I spy a couple of taxis whizzing past, their drivers *wai*ing, their hands off the wheel, their heads turned completely in the direction of the shrine, their tourist passengers looking horrified, their faces contorted into Munch's *Scream*.

The shrine is a blaze of purple-and-yellow flowers and sweetly pungent smoke. Four girls in bright make-up and national costume, blue, green and gold-sequinned headdresses and jangly golden jewellery are dancing and singing the praises of a generous donor.

'Meesta Teema! Meesta Teema! Nice man! Nice man!'

I decide it's time my luck changed. I give plenty of money and explain my story. They look baffled and then sing the version they understand.

'Mrs Clah! His cat? Mrs Clah! He dead! Mrs Clah!'

For some reason it's not as comforting as I had hoped.

TWELVE

CHIANG MAI

FED UP WITH the stink, the noise and the crowds of the Village of Plums, I head for Chiang Mai, where I hope to hit Ed Rose's cattery, next on Martin's list. Before leaving, Dodie, who has more shopping to do in Bangkok, invites me to stay with her at the Regent, Chiang Mai's flashest hotel, in a few days' time.

The train leaves Hua Lampong station, and pulls out through shanty towns of people living on the tracks, their homes iron-roofed huts, with neon strips for lighting, earthen floors and smoking stoves, their washing hung on lines. Outside the huts are fairy lights on shrines, inches from the train's path. The train is air-conditioned and clean. Dinner and breakfast are served.

The guard comes and makes the large bunks with clean sheets and pillows and warm, just steamed blankets, fresh from the laundry like newly baked bread. The couple in the next-door bunk are Thai – he very old, she very young. The second the beds are made they get in and close the curtains and start giggling. Then she starts making 'mmm, mmm' noises. Trains are so exciting.

I'm right next to the people who want to talk all night.

I wish they'd simmer down so I could listen to the engine. The woman next door is regaling me with a volley of snores. Loneliness creeps in around my edges. Considering the number of times this has happened I should be used to it by now, and yet somehow I'm not. Every time it feels like cold coffee being tipped down my back. Oh my heavy heart.

Finally I dream. A woman tears back the dividing curtain, her face and body silhouettes against the glaring white of the eternal light strip. She lays her hands on my arm but instead of hands or even ghastly stumps are huge hairy tarantulas, their legs waving one after the other like sea anemones in the clean tide. Argh!

Chiang Mai is Thailand's second city. King Mengrai chose the city in 1292 to be the capital of his Lanna kingdom when he got bored with Chiang Rai. It was a major base for Theravada Buddhism: although forty-five times smaller than Bangkok it has almost the same number of *wats*. Wandering around, I feel slightly watted out, and so organise myself a tour.

Soon I am heading for the hills between Chiang Mai and Chiang Rai. Sometimes they are so close they seem like woolly green waves just outside the window. We bump over a dirt track for miles, that clings to the side of a mountain. I feel a twinge of terror as the car skids round the corner, one wheel whizzing off one side of the mountain, rocks scattering down the sheer drop below.

I'm staying at a lodge that looks over the mountains to

pink-and-blue clouds and the expanse of the wooded hills. There are two other girls already there, Helena and Sponge (Sponge? *Hello?*). Helena looks like a Thai Liv Tyler. She is warm, open, intelligent, lovely. I develop a crush on her almost immediately. Sponge is portly with cherubic blond curls.

We want to trek across the valley so we ask our driver which way to go.

He replies, 'You *farang* always like to walk. Why not take the car?'

I really can't fault his argument. *Farang* is the Thai word for foreigners. It also manages to imply moose-like stupidity. Which seems apt considering we are trekking, or bombing to be more precise, up a hill in the mid-day heat.

Sponge strides forth in her sarong past a slash-and-burn farmer wearing a Coca-Cola T-shirt. Both Helena and Sponge have studied for eco-friendly MAs at SOAS but only Sponge is pro-nature, organics and the environment. Helena, when confronted by a centipede the size of a comb chugging by, or a worm the length of a cinema aisle, yells, 'Gross!' and bombs off in the other direction.

'Oh but they're lovely!' says Sponge and, 'They're so sweet,' of ants the size of armchairs when they bite into the worm, causing it to writhe in agony in its attempt to get away. We are pouring sweat.

'Ah, I could tape the sounds of the countryside,' continues Sponge.

Just at that moment an electric organ sounds across

the valley from the temple. It plays 'London Bridge is Falling Down' and over the next few hours will play more fab techno toons like 'Congratulations', 'Popeye the Sailor Man', Alan Freeman's Pop Pickers and the New World Symphony just before it bongs a tinny version of Big Ben.

Back at the lodge Helena and I discuss our lives. Her mother died recently and she is deciding which job to do. I am searching for the perfect cat. The light fades. While we discuss boyfriends and dead mothers, we smoke and eat chocolate biscuits and Thai sweets of jelly with solidified coconut milk, wrapped in tiny banana leaves.

'Listen,' she whispers after a while. 'Do you want to try something new after supper?'

Memories of Maria in Burma float up scarily.

'Er, perhaps?'

After dinner, she leads Sponge and me up the hill to the hut of an old man, whose sunken emaciated cheeks make his profession clear. We take it in turns to lie down next to him, in the glow of a candle. He then prises off a bit of the opium, burns it over a flame, moulds it with his long-blackened fingers and pokes it into the pipe. I inhale, scared I'll be instantly sick, or addicted, or both. The smoke is very sweet, it doesn't induce the usual fight against nature to overcome the pain. The bubbles mount and encroach on the hole. We then sit in the darkness near the fire taking turns to have more. I'm alive and happy. Falling asleep is a lovely slide into oblivion where the line between sleep and life moves so that I encounter dreams so potent they seem real.

Next day, though still heavily drugged, I'm dying for more. For a moment I'm bemused as to why it's illegal, and why the Princess Mother, the King of Thailand's mother, went to so much trouble to turn the opium-producing hills of northern Thailand into cash-crop producers.

'Why is it illegal?' I ask Helena. 'Why doesn't everyone smoke it? How could anyone fight when feeling like this? It's so peaceful.'

'Shall I get a bucket of cold water for you?' she replies. 'You sound like a bloody hippie.'

All day we loll around chatting, smoking, drinking, eating nothing. The temperature is hot, but not boiling like down in the city. And at night there is a delicious coolness in the air as though a fridge door has been opened. Once evening has drawn in again, we meander back up the hill. It takes us double the time it did last night.

Lying on the bed again, we inhale the pipes. Opium is unlike other drugs, in that you don't feel hyper or jittery or sleepy or hungry, and your mind stays the same. It doesn't get paranoid or meander through mazes of thoughts unable to wend its way back to the original idea afterwards. You feel normal. Which I feel very rarely anyway so it's a welcome relief.

We move to our beds slowly and dreamily, under the moon which is so bright it might be dawn. The stars move like white insects against a smoky night sky. I spend the night swimming on soft mattresses holding hands with Cat

Cam Man who disappears in a puff of smoke just before dawn. Next morning I realise that getting stoned, though lovely, is hardly the most efficient way of finding my cat. So I head back for Chiang Mai.

A tuk tuk delivers me to Ed and Malee's cattery on the outskirts of Chiang Mai. In spite of the fact that the driver swears blind he knows where it is, and he protests there isn't a corner of Chiang Mai he doesn't know, we have to stop and ask five people the way once we hit the outskirts. At one point we find we have missed our turning off a motorway, so, undaunted, the driver turns round and drives the wrong way back down the motorway and down a one-way feed-in road. Terrifying.

Set well back from the road a large house displaying 'We Love Siamese' stickers is lined with cages containing masses and masses of Siamese, Burmese, and Khorats (another Thai breed, sleek and silver-blue in colour with green eyes).

Admiring his cats, I ask Ed how old they are.

'Apparently the traditional Siamese cat existed in Ayutthaya, Siam's ancient capital city, as early as 1350.'

'Actually I meant how old is this one?'

'Oh! She's nine months.'

'And were they really royal cats? Were they kept exclusively in royal palaces?'

'I don't know. Although I believe that when the young King of Siam was crowned in 1926 a white cat was carried by the court chamberlains in the procession to the Throne Room as a sign of reverence for the departed monarch. But that was because, being Buddhist, the Siamese believed in the transmigration of souls. Traditional Siamese cats were kept with great care in the King's palace as resting places for royal souls. When a member of the Royal House of Siam was buried, one of his favourite cats would be entombed with him. The burial chamber would have holes in the roof, which a clever cat could escape from. In fact when it did, the people took this as a sign that the dead person's soul was now successfully reincarnated in the cat.'

But swaggering around outside, as if to say 'Oh *forget* the Siamese cat's history – look at *me*!' and flaunting his freedom in front of the caged cats, is a Claudius *doppelgänger*. Exactly the same colour as Claudius, milk-chocolate-brown, he even has a few white hairs on his chest like Claude. His face is not quite as beautiful, being a little more angular, but he exudes that air of owning the world. His name is Chum – pronounced halfway between Chum and Choom. His favourite trick is to jump up the front of Ed's trousers. Chum is incredibly friendly and shows me around the other cages full of healthy, lively cats. But he doesn't say a word.

I wonder if it's the language difference but then realise I'm being ridiculous as Cat is a separate language from Thai. I try all my most polite phrases, somewhat rusty, since I haven't spoken Cat properly since Claudius was alive, but Chum responds neither to 'What would Chum like for dinner tonight?' or 'Does Chum like a goose eiderdown to sleep on?' (In Cat the human always addresses the animal in the third person as a mark of respect, no matter how close they may be. Claudius and I were like brother and sister, but to the very end of his life when speaking Cat I always referred to him as 'he'.)

As a result of Chum's silence, I'm not sure whether to buy him or not. I feel sure that if we're meant for each other he'll recognise me too. Nevertheless I ask Ed how much he is. $400 is the reply.

'Blimey,' slips out before I can stop it.

Breeding the cats more for a hobby than a living, Ed is uninterested in indulging me in my newly acquired bargaining skills.

Telling him I'll think about it, I make my way to the Regent to meet Dodie, where I am greeted with jasmine garlands and bowls of fruit punch in a large open wooden reception area lit with candles, smelling of frangipani and looking out on to emerald rice paddies and navy mountains. I gawp but Dodie swans over to say hello. She is used to this. It is her due.

She is in platforms, trousers, a see-through dress, a Pucci shirt and a Florida-style crownless sunshade cap. She even has a leopardskin eye mask around her neck in case she feels like taking a nap midday (in a restaurant sitting up, perhaps?). She looks, in short, insane. She's also got a Louis Vuitton bag on her shoulder. (Although I notice her handbag is stuffed full of toiletries and writing paper nicked from the Oriental in Bangkok. I *love* the fact she is not quite able to shake off her suburban roots.)

Outside, geckos shoot up the whitewashed walls like twisting ladders. Our room has a domed wooden ceiling with a bed big enough for a family of ten. Our balcony stretches into the distance. The bath is the size of a pool. Everything is spotless. It is heaven. At night the pool is lit by huge urns with fire leaping from them. The edges are seamless, so the water continues flowing over them. The gardens are lit by large candles. We order room service and revel in American food – Reuben sandwich (beef, sauerkraut and cheese) and a hamburger with fries. Then we watch a movie. I love the protection of this total luxury – the cleanliness, the fresh smells, the comfort.

'I wonder where my new cat is,' I whisper in the night, but Dodie is already asleep with a red satin eye mask on her eyes, 'Dream' written on it in *diamanté*.

When they ask me to leave this place I'm going to handcuff myself to the bed. I'm never leaving. Ever. Although I must admit it is quite strange being here with a near stranger, accepting her hospitality and sleeping in the bed with her.

'I agree,' says a voice to my left, which makes me jump a mile into the air.

'Who is it?'

'Who do you think it is?' says Claude, a large brown foggy blob in the armchair opposite.

'Claude? Claude! What are you doing here?'

'I'm dummy so I thought I'd pop in and say hello.'

'You're dummy? What are you talking about?'

'I'm playing bridge with Mata Hari, Mummy and Michelangelo.'

'Michelangelo?'

'Yes, it took us ages to teach him, he simply had no concept of cards for a while, but eventually we did it.'

'And you?'

'What about me?'

I don't like to point out he's a cat, as this always used to wind him up, so I just say, 'Well, I was wondering how you held the cards without opposable thumbs.'

'Hah!' he snorts as if I know nothing. 'I don't need those. They just hover.'

With that he jumps down from the armchair as if 'hover' is enough explanation. He looks strange, larger than life.

'Claude?'

'Mmm?'

He's rubbing his whiskers against a particularly fine Burmese wood carving.

'Are you wearing clothes?'

'This old thing?' he says, pointing to a rather exquisite smoking jacket. 'Oh I just throw this on any old time.'

He turns away smiling, glad I've noticed. It's worthy of Oscar Wilde, so rich is the velvet, so beautiful the colours.

'Now what are you doing here?' he asks, looking around the intensely luxurious room.

'Ah yes, well, you see, I . . .' I say sheepishly.

'The craving and then the achievement of this sort of luxury is never going to bring happiness.'

He looks round once more, then settles down in the sphinx position (in the most comfortable chair, I notice), somewhat creasing his jacket as he does so, and then closes his eyes.

'Anything you are fervently wishing to have, *anything*, mind you, is not the answer. Once you have it, it'll merely be replaced by some other desire.'

He opens his eyes momentarily, widens the jet in the jade of his eyes and closes them again promptly.

'The point is that this desire makes you unhappy. But you can free yourself from it by following a few precepts.'

He suddenly looks round as though he's seen a bird.

'Oh *bugger*,' he says, and disappears in a puff of smoke.

Which is very annoying as I have a million questions for him, not least a message for my mother. What can he mean?

I sleep soundly until morning. Well, until 5 a.m. when Dodie wakes up and starts doing yoga in bed.

Walking out of the shower, I bump into Dodie, and scream, because her face apart from the eyes and mouth is covered in a bright-green face mask. She peruses the stripped me. She purses her lips and cocks her eyebrows.

'It's an absolute must.'

'What is?'

'A Brazilian.'

'A what?'

'A Brazilian. The type of wax treatment all the girls in New York have.'

'What is it?'

227

'Well, they wax everything apart from a nodule above the mons Veneris. I mean everything. Behind, between, around.'

'Ouch. *Ouch*. Stop it. Don't tell me these things. I don't need to know.'

'I understand your fear. There's no fear like the first time. It's addictive afterwards though. Personally I used to have this tweezing addiction.'

She pauses.

'I get mine done at J Sisters. That's where everyone goes.'

Dodie looks so Thai with her long black hair and black eyes that sometimes I forget that she's never going to say anything submissive and respectful. She pulls open an enormous closet with brightly lit full-length mirrors.

'Good God! I didn't realise I was a Renoir bathing beauty,' she says in Betty Grable pose, inspecting her bottom. 'I know men think women are vain, but looking in this mirror isn't a sign of narcissism, ya know. I don't expect a new ass, just something a little better than last time. You get away to see who you are in the rear-view mirror,' she adds quietly.

Admittedly our conversations aren't always the most intellectual. But now and then they are.

'Have you read *Wings of the Dove*?'

'No.'

'Me neither. But I've seen the film. Do you remember that bit when she's sure the heiress will leave her money to the guy?'

'No.'

'And he says how do you know and she says because that's the way she loves?'

'No.'

'Well anyway, it's the same thing with me. I mean how do you love?'

And I can't reply, because recently I've not given myself the chance.

I don't know whether to let Dodie in on the secret that I've been having visions of my dead cat in a smoking jacket. Not today perhaps. We plonk ourselves by the incredible infinity pool and watch the boys working with the buffalo in the rice paddies. They look suspiciously like dressed-up RADA-trained actors but the brochure assures me they *and* the buffalo are fully paid-up members of staff. Claudius has made me feel a bit guilty about all this luxury – which is very annoying of him, as luxury like this is, well, fantastic.

Dodie is obsessed with massages. So we go to the local blind school to be kneaded by boys with sliding boiled-egg whites instead of eyes, as though God had forgotten to give them pupils. It's a beauty parlour come slumber party with mattresses lined up next to each other on the floor. There is a sign in the loo saying 'Please do not wash feet in toilet'. As if. The boys pray to Buddha first at a little shrine in the corner of the room with jasmine rings and baskets of bright yellow-and-pink flowers as offerings. My masseur burps copiously throughout the massage but I don't hold this against him.

'Breathe, breathe, breathe,' instructs Dodie.

She is in her high-heeled wedges, black skirt, white T-shirt, green Jackie O specs, brown lipstick and brown toe polish. Most suitable, considering it's raining so hard outside the tuk tuk boys have white plastic covers on their heads. They look like psychedelic brides on bikes.

Thai massage is more full-on than Swedish massage. The masseur uses his feet, hands, legs, arms, elbows, anything he feels will really do the job. He wraps his legs around you, digs his knees into your back, his elbows into your ears.

Dodie is also obsessed with elephants and in New York bought some 'elephant art' ($300 at a Christie's auction, which surely shows more money than sense) painted by an elephant from the Young Elephant Training Centre in Lampang. Dying to meet this young genius, we head south.

Immediately we see an enormous elephant beside her tiny baby – the sweetest little thing smaller than a large dog – being fed bananas and sugar cane by tourists. The sound of her crunching the entire sugar cane, bark coat and all, is very satisfying. Foul, hideous, out-of-tune music like screeching dead violins sliding up and down the scale emanates from a local instrument further up the hill where there are more elephants. I pay the musician to stop.

'I have the urge to dress it up in fanciful costumes,' says Dodie of the nearest elephant, who follows his friends down to the lake for a bath.

The elephants have lovely long eyelashes, but the smell. Boy, do they smell. They need that lake. Their skin is incredibly rough with dark spots on a browny-beige background. The mahouts go in with them to give them a good scrub. The nellies love it, and splosh around lumberingly.

Then sitting on the elephants' necks the mahouts trundle them up the hill to the show ground. The elephants walk in holding each other's tails – so sweet! They roll logs and pick them up and play the xylophone and paint on white paper. They produce nutty pictures of colourful strokes. After each trick the elephant bows and we clap loudly. As for the mahouts, the tradition is passed down from father to son. There are no female mahouts, which is one of those maddening Southeast Asian traditions that no woman seems to want to break.

The mahouts climb up with the help of the elephant's bent front leg. They then use a baton behind the ears to control the elephant. When the mahout drops the baton, the elephant 'returns its tool of oppression to its master', as Dodie puts it.

Asian elephants are smaller than African elephants and have smaller ears. On average they weigh 35,000 kilos while the average African elephant weighs 47,000 kilos. Only the males have tusks. They do not like cats or dogs or anything that's faster than they are. They sleep on their sides and they yawn and snore. Each day they eat 150–200 kilos of leaves, grass, bark, sugar cane and bananas. They can drag logs weighing up to half their own body weight. They spend eighteen hours eating and four hours sleeping.

'Why do the young elephants paint?' I ask a girl working at the centre.

Luckily she is honest enough not to say, 'It's their innate artistic talent,' or some such bullshit, but instead replies sweetly, 'Oh we needed new ways of making money for the centre. So we thought we'd give them paintbrushes.'

I keep this mum from Dodie.

A little kerfuffle in the corner indicates Dodie needs my help.

'I'm caught in some kind of snafu,' she says wearily. 'They want me to take a picture of this elephant and then pay for it.'

She shakes her head despairingly.

'Picture, picture,' the mahout shouts excitedly, pointing at his charge.

'Actually I think that's the artist you're looking for,' I reply.

'*Oh*. My. *God!*' she squeals excitedly and flings her arms around the elephant, causing the mahout to look alarmed and the elephant to execute a quick trunk-search over her body for hidden bananas.

Yes, in front of us is none other than the surprisingly named, yet artistically famous, Bird. And I quote from the Christie's auction book of the Asian Elephant Art and Conservation Project:

Reckless and impulsive, Bird is a born artist. The

night before classes began at the Ayuthaya Academy, Bird could barely restrain his enthusiasm. After the trainers had gone to sleep he broke into one of the storerooms and stealthily prised the lid off one of the cans of paint that had been set aside for the first lesson. He couldn't find a brush so he improvised, dipping his trunk into the can and smearing the camp's buildings and corrals with sloppy streaks of cobalt blue. Like many elephant artists, Bird was born into a family of timber workers, and the brute physicality of his working-class background informs much of his painting. Bird approaches a blank canvas with a potent combination of exhilaration and fury, swinging his trunk in broad, sweeping strokes, forward and back as if painting a fence. When he wants to change colour he tosses the brush on to the ground and impatiently waits for a new one. His paintings with their broad tectonic lines of black, dark blue and forest green have often drawn comparisons to the work of Abstract Expressionist painter Franz Kline.

Bonkers. Absolutely nuts.

Dodie heads back to the Regent. Unfortunately I cannot shift the vague haze of guilt that envelops me every time I settle into an overly plump chair or lower my boiling body into the cool heavenliness of the pool, so I tell Dodie that I'm going for a few days to Mae Sot. She holds her hands straight up with the thumbs just touching at a 45-degree angle: Whatever.

'Let's meet up when you're ready to move on,' she drawls.

I head for Mae Sot.

THIRTEEN

MAE SOT TO PHUKET TO HUA HIN TO BANGKOK

THROUGH MIST TO grey to vivid white the plane (whose fare cost me just £10) climbs closer to the light. Below are rice fields like the pieces of a child's jigsaw puzzle, huge and unwieldy, and mountains like the bodies of sleeping elephants. A golden river winds before them to the border of Burma. The idyllic rural scene belies the fighting and upset on the land – the Thais unhappy with the large number of refugees spilling over into their territory, the Burmese unwilling to let any dissenting Burmese live and walk free.

Mae Sot is a small frontier town with dusty wide streets and quiet markets selling Wellington boots and straw hats. Many of the shopkeepers are gem traders and this is the main reason I am here, as Mogok in Burma was closed to visitors. I eat dinner in a restaurant open to the road, where the cats have kinked and broken tails. These are unfriendly, untrusting creatures, used to a life of scrabbling and fighting for everything they get. One has a tail actually tied in knots. Cat people I speak to continually assure me the tail thing is genetic, which I can't quite believe. I have yet to see a normal cat on the street with a normal tail.

I smell. My Buddhist belief in simplicity and packing lightly actually translates into a lack of change of clothes, so in order to avoid nakedness, I wash my clothes rarely. Now, if I were to bottle the odour of myself and my clothes, I'd make a fortune in paint stripper. Meanwhile a dog is fascinated by the smell of my shoes. This is hardly surprising, as being trainers (actually very trendy blue-and-yellow Nike Air Rifts which young Thais all stare at with undisguised, unmitigated envy), they have developed an aroma so strong that when I take them off they quite often follow me for a step or two. (Have I yet mentioned the dogs of Southeast Asia? An uglier, scrappier set of smelly, hairless, pus-infested, woundy hounds I have never seen. They are all terrified of humans, slinking off with their tails between their legs before I even get the chance to give them a gentle, subtle kick out of my way. They are terrified of life.) Soon the dog is joined by a couple more, and, stared at by many laughing Thais, I wend my way back, followed by a rapidly growing string of dogs.

At the hotel I am able to shut them out. But oh how gloomy it is. Run by men, the hotel is noisy and full of shuffling, staring, sinister men slamming doors and shouting in the echoey corridors. The walls are grey and dirty. The curtains are yellow and threadbare. The neon strips of light reveal greying sheets. The floor tiles are mottled. The pillow smells musty. The floor has ominous holes that could belch out cockroaches at any time. The smell of drains from the bathroom hits the back of my throat like bleach.

Out of the window things are better. There is a temple with mountains in the distance. Its sleeping gold twinkles now and then from the reflection of fairy lights sailing aft to the top. Crickets chirp outside and a monk sings through the temple's loudspeaker. I am yearning for more, more, more, some depth, some reality, something. My recent skirmishes with cats are not providing it. The guy next door is farting like a firecracker.

Then the phone rings.

'Hello?'

'Hello?'

'Hello?'

'Hello?'

Not seeing the potential of this conversation I gently put the phone down. But it rings again.

'I see you.'

'Who is this?'

'I see you in street. I like your shoes. I follow you to hotel.'

'Er, are you a *dog*?'

'I describe you and they phone you.'

'That's the last time I stay here, I guess, then.'

'You very lovely. I luff yew. I good boy. I handsome boy. I take you to cinema.'

'No. No, you don't take me to cinema. I don't want to know you, you stalking loony.'

'Solly? I luff yew.'

'You can't love me. You don't know me.'

I say this with a tone of 'Of course you do, but . . .' at which point I realise my vanity has the better of me.

'Do you have boyfriend?'

'*Yes!*' I realise this is the key to my freedom. 'I do.'

'Does he lib in the room with you?'

'*Yes!* He lives right here with me. *Darling!* He's in the bathroom. I'll get him for you.'

A dead line. It's a shame that *my* wishes are unheeded and only when I am the property of somebody else does he call off the hunt. But as I put the phone down it occurs to me that this room would be less miserable if there *were* a boyfriend taking a shower in the drain-ridden bathroom. We could then laugh about the ridiculous hotel. And if it were Cat Cam Man, the room would seem absolutely lovely.

At first I think the call is quite funny. But after realising that if he got this far he could probably talk reception into giving my room number as well, I worry that he'll come up to my room. I'd like to go out but, for the first time in a long time, I feel threatened. Actually I might have met him had his English been good enough – it might have been interesting (being chopped to death in some back alley). If he comes up here I'll kill the receptionist. If I'm still alive to do it, that is.

After five minutes I get up the courage to go downstairs to her. She speaks no English and my Thai is not appropriate here so my arms speak the international language of disapproval. She gets the gist. Not nice to think that as I walk down the street eyes are watching and feet are following.

Dreadful tinny pop music is issuing from the temple now. The song is horribly long and loud. It is like trying to sleep in a disco but there is absolutely nothing I can do about it. Then when it stops I worship the silence, dreading the racket's imminent return, and sure enough after a few moments another horrid noise starts up. I wonder how the locals put up with it and if it interferes with their TV-watching. Perhaps they like it and sway along happily, knowing the entire community is also forced to listen, thereby deriving some sort of tinny unity.

The deadly dull of insomnia – my heavy, sleepless head in the black. This fantastic energy would be amazing if only it would present itself during the day rather than at night. I could have created companies! Learnt languages! Achieved degrees at night!

To calm myself down I imagine Claudius's brown tail swinging like a furry pendulum in front of my eyes, hypnotising me to sleep.

'Perhaps you may have worked out,' he says, 'that since this immense dissatisfaction with everything around you has risen, so it can abate too.'

'I am *so* dissatisfied,' I reply dozily. 'Why is this?'

'Because you're always wanting. Wanting the perfect cat. And trying to change things. Change the temple music, change the receptionist's behaviour, change this, change that. Rather than accepting reality as it is. It's ironic. Because when things *do* change you don't accept them.'

'What sort of change don't I accept?'

'My death, for instance. The end of your relationships.'

'Who says I don't accept them?'

'Well then, why are you trying to turn back time by finding a replica of me?'

I'm silent.

'You are constantly desiring things, aren't you?' he continues, his tail actually starting to tickle the end of my nose until I start sneezing. 'Packing very few things only works if you don't then hanker after spangly nail varnish. *N'est-ce pas?*'

His tail is now performing psychedelic patterns like Kaa's eyes in front of mine.

'How about some advice then?' emanates from my closed eyelids.

'Well, we can work towards ending dissatisfaction by freeing the mind – by attaining nirvana. Firstly, realise that everything is *change*, must change, that nothing is rigid. And secondly try to lose yourself – be part of the bigger picture. Do something selfless . . . And try the eightfold path, through which one can attain nirvana. The first point is right view: this means not holding on to any particular view of reality because that freezes it, which doesn't allow for the inherent flexibility of the world. Take Dick Whittington, for instance. He may have had a cat, then again he may have been a merchant who sold favours, known as achats – a-cats. You see? There is more than one view on the matter, and who knows which is right. The second point on the path is right – and by right I don't mean right as in the dualistic concept of right and wrong or right and left –'

'What do you mean then?'

'I just mean "right"!' he snaps. 'The second point is right intention. The third point is right speech. Not lying. Not speaking crudely or rudely, not speaking ill of others and refraining from gossip.'

But by this stage I am gently snoring.

As I explore Mae Sot looking for cats, a girl buying flowers in the market says hello, and asks me where I'm from. I'm super friendly, because her English is good and I'd love some company. At first we wander down dusty streets, but then we seem to be walking in a definite direction.

'Where are we going?'

'This way to where I live,' Sawe replies, looking ahead.

Once there I find myself surrounded by Burmese Karen women, each illegally out of a border camp. A German girl is working here as a volunteer, her hair in a bun, tiny circular glasses on the end of her nose, like a nineteenth-century missionary. The women offer me Karen food, rice with a spicy curry and greens. The German girl eats hers with her fingers, messing up her rice and curry into a ball and popping it in her mouth, while the Karen girls all eat with wide steel spoons. Ah how the East loves the West and the West loves the East.

Sawe tells me of refugees being sent back to Burma where they are killed for having left.

'We know girls who have been raped by their Thai employers and the army do nothing,' she says slowly, pausing, searching for the right word. 'Four of our girls were promised work in Mae Sot but the trafficker who took them deposited them in a Muslim house where none of the girls were paid – but were beaten with heavy logs

241

and boots, kicked and used as slaves. They were captive for three years. One girl died. When they were finally freed, one girl's face was so badly scarred she was ashamed and refused to return to the camp. But another returned, but she is now mad in the head. She jumps if you even call her name. She says they had long nails attached to their fingers which they used to stab into the girls' mouths. They were locked in their room for hours on end and not allowed to go to the loo or have enough to eat.'

Thinking that I might be able to help in some way, however mundane, I ask Sawe to take me to the refugee camp where her family lives. Perhaps there is something I can do for them. The trip involves several hours' ride in a pickup truck winding so high into the mountains we touch the clouds. I sit up front with another girl and we share our purchases from the roadside stops: corn on the cob and sticky sweets. Every time we stop Sawe is violently sick – poor thing – which is not surprising considering the curves and the hard benches in the back of the pickup and the number of people crammed on to them. There are so many of us, everyone apart from myself travelling illegally, that the pickup is almost at a standstill, revving and roaring away on some of the inclines. At shanty towns we stop to let on even more people.

The camp itself is incredibly well organised. Neat rows of bamboo houses cover the hill. Bamboo steps form a road between the rows all the way to the top. The houses have little gardens growing spring onions and eucalyptus and tamarind trees. Cats and dogs and chickens are hanging around outside the huts. There is a hospital and a church and a school with swings, slides and see-saws. But this carefully tended, seemingly tranquil spot, like all refugee camps, is burnt down now and then by either the Thai or the Burmese armies. Then the families have to start all over again buying bamboo, because they are not allowed to chop down any teak, and building their houses. It is a miserable existence.

Now in Sawe's family hut, I am freezing cold, dirty and beaten by fleas. Sawe is incredibly kind, giving me three thin (but valuable) candles, although I am not allowed to burn them after 8 p.m. Nor are we allowed a fire. The hut has stairs down to a kitchen area and stairs down to an outside squat loo where there is also a barrel containing freezing water for washing. Sawe's family do nothing all day and it doesn't take long to realise that, if they have nothing to do, I'll have nothing to do either and my desire to help won't do much good. Sawe's younger brother and sister spend hours huddled around a radio and sing along to all the songs – her brother has a very good voice. At night, soft singing issues from several of the huts nearby, ghostly lullabies on the grey velvet breeze.

In the night, endless rain comes through the roof dripping on to my musty blanket. I am on a hard floor and dying of cold, my pashmina wrapped around my head. By morning my eyes are very painful. Every time I close and move them I see white cartoon eye shapes. My back is so stiff, the next few days will be hobblesome.

In the morning a ginger kitten with its entire tail is in the kitchen. I feed it sardines, a welcome break from its usual rice fare – and afterwards it settles on my tummy to sleep, its purrs vibrating through my loins.

'It belongs to my father,' says Sawe.

'Why do so many cats have knots in their tails? Is it genetic?'

'No. People do it to stop other people stealing their cat. It is a sign of ownership. But my father doesn't like it so he left the kitten's tail alone.'

Today I meet the camp leaders. They face many difficulties. The camp has a drug problem amongst the bored young men, who buy cheap amphetamines brought in from Burma.

'The SPDC fights us in many ways,' says the camp deputy leader, 'with weapons, but also with drugs and religion. They want to divide us so they have created the DKBA (the Democratic Karen Buddhist Army) to fight the KNU (Karen National Union). The SPDC uses the DKBA to get into the camp and sell drugs here.'

We're sitting around a large wooden table in a hut right on top of the mountain. Milling around outside are monster dogs with bulging and bloody eyes. Now and then the odd hacking noise, from both men and women, clearing their throats of phlegm and snot, wafts through the wooden walls, making me feel slightly queasy. The clouds are all around us – a fog of light. It's cold and wet and miserable.

'We want to organise a drug-treatment centre. We always have to be prepared and cautious. There is a plan to destroy the camp but so far nothing has happened. But the worst thing that could happen to us would be forced repatriation. This is a continual worry. Our villages have all been destroyed by the Burmese army and if we went back we would surely be killed.'

Sawe's mother works with the Women's Group. They organise the orphanage and the planting of gardens for vegetables. They generate income through weaving and sewing. They run workshops on accountancy, power-sharing and repatriation. Dressed in lungis and Oxfam clothes (tracksuit jackets, thin multicoloured jumpers, Clark's shoes and sandals), they joke and laugh, even though they've spent their lives watching their husbands get killed like dogs in the street, escaping from their villages into the mountains, portering for the SPDC in land-mined country and moving from camp to camp hounded by the Burmese army. And that's not even counting the rape. Or the loss. Once in Thailand they lose all contact with the rest of their families, because the families get beaten or jailed if the SPDC thinks they're communicating. Their faces are covered in yellow *thanakha* paste, their black shiny hair tied neatly in plaits or bunches.

'We want our children to have a future and a chance for education,' Sawe's mother explains to me. 'In the refugee camp they can only go to grade 10 – there's no chance for further studies. There are schools near towns but the Karen state schools are all closed, and there is no education in the deep jungle, or for the borderline people. When in Thailand we become the enemy. We don't have enough money for candles, soap and medicine for the children. Yet we'd like to be able to give them meat twice a week and vegetables at every meal.

'My friends have endured unbearable hardships. Cho La had to give a child away at birth because she didn't have enough money to feed him. Her husband had been shot in the mouth by the SPDC. She lived under a plastic shelter for three months after her camp was destroyed by the SPDC. The soldiers are terrifying. They beat the least resistance savagely. A whole day's work in the fields earned them just one cup of rice. The men the SPDC kill are simple men with no political contacts at all. The villages are constantly attacked and burned. These people walk through the jungle for weeks to get here. They don't have enough to eat so they eat berries or anything they can find in the forest. Then when we get here we cannot leave the camp or work. And we don't have work permits or legal papers.'

She introduces me to a seventeen-year-old girl who answers my questions in monosyllables, her eyes continually downcast. She watched her mother being gunned down by the SPDC when she was five. She was standing next to her, hiding behind a boulder.

'They were ransacking the village and killed anyone indiscriminately. There were no schools. So I came to Thailand by myself a year ago. I haven't heard from my family since. I walked with seven other people but we didn't have enough food. We were hungry. We walked for a month through the jungle. I followed a friend.'

Her life has been beaten out of her. I cry but my tears are useless.

Back at the hut, as the sky darkens from blue to navy, Sawe and her sister prepare dinner. Her sister is wearing a green cloth folded on her head like Cleopatra. I sweep the floor. The only conversation I have had that does not involve random killings, rape, lost babies and forced marches through land mines was with Sawe's English teacher. A small wizened old guy, the moment he learnt I was English, he broke into a discourse on the weather.

Night. Once again I'm trussed up like a Romanian peasant attempting to beat off the cold. The scuffling above my head must be rats. I read by candlelight. When the candle dies, the last flame, shaped like a golden nail, diminishes to a blue blob before spluttering out. Then I lie freezing in the darkness. I am behind my curtained-off area, lying on my back with the cat nestled in my joints, thinking of absolutely nothing, because if I think about what I've been told during the day, I cry. But it doesn't work. Soon I get angry. And with good reason as I remember my conversation with the 'King of Burma'. It makes me livid to think the Burmese government has defenders, people trying to 'deblacken the generals' name'. There's very good reason for the generals' reputation of dirt. The tourist routes don't show the real situation, and travellers shouldn't be fooled by them.

The one comfort is the ginger kitten who warms me up like a hot-water bottle. This reminds me of Winston Churchill's comment about his black cat Nelson, whom he allowed to sleep with him every night. He said Nelson was helping the war effort by saving on heating costs.

Each hour of the night is marked out on hollow bamboo sticks. Each different area of the camp beats its echoing raindrop toc toc, a few seconds apart. It is comforting to know that time is passing. The cocks start crowing non-stop at 3.30 a.m. – like Red Indians screeching war cries.

Back in Mae Sot, ready to move on, I stop at one of the many gem dealer's in town, not wanting to leave without a jewel. Let's just say that when I left the building, more than one man was rubbing his chin, shaking his head and laughing. I won't think about at whose expense they were laughing. Suffice to say the recipient of this ruby will be mighty pleased, I am sure.

From Mae Sot, I fly to Phuket to meet up with Dodie. At the airport, I amuse myself on the massage chairs, which wobble and make one's chest do things that normally people pay to see.

'I never see beauty in nature as lovely as what I see on the Discovery Channel,' says Dodie, describing her flight over the rugged terrain heading south.

Looking for somewhere to stay Dodie tries her Memphis drawl on random passers-by.

'Do you know a guest house nearby?'

'Um?'

'A guest house?'

'Guess how?'

'Guest house?' She pauses. 'Do you know the square root

of pi? Do you know the meaning of life? Might as well ask them the biggies as they have no concept of the smalls,' she murmurs to herself.

Finally she opts for an enormous Florida-style faceless hotel, with lots of fleshy English girls in too short, too tight dresses with their hair in corn rows. Everyone is pink and sunburned. Dodie does not seem overly impressed. She's used to better things because her allowance is similar to Britain's annual defence budget. We head into Phuket.

Phuket was more appropriately named by its early traders – Junkceylon. The difference between the refugee camp and this is ridiculous. Now this former banana plantation is a hideous conglomerate of McDonald's, Starbuck's, Tower Records, with everything grossly overpriced and men hassling you on the street to go into their tailor shops. We look at endless Gucci Fendi Prada fakes, silk cushion covers, burgundy sarongs with golden elephants, tie-dye dresses. There's no sign of Thailand here.

'I love your hair,' I say to an elderly stallholder, whose short black crop lies close to her crown.

'An old Thai custom at my age,' she replies.

'Oh really?'

'In tribute to the sisters who saved Phuket from the Burmese in 1785. One was the widow of the governor who just died. They cut their hair short and roasted coconut-palm leaves until black and curled, and then ran among their own army and made terrible noises to make the army look bigger. Then they sneaked back to the city late at night and marched out again so the Burmese thought the army was very *very* big. Older women cut their hair short to be strong and resourceful like them.'

'It's good to know there are some old traditions in this town.'

'Yes, some old traditions not as good as others,' she says, looking at a tiny woman in a bandeau top and platforms wandering arm in arm with an enormous, beer-bellied muscly guy in a string vest and with a footballer's haircut.

Outside one bar, huge screens project MTV with its dancing girls, all primped and mascaraed and preened and loads of make-up and flowing hair and very sexy and perfect. My brain rots watching it. Want the TV off, I want the air-conditioner off, I want the lights off, I want the streets cleared of people. I hate it here.

Back in the silence of the hotel room, I hear the gentle burr of purr on the breeze, gradually increasing like the sound of an approaching biplane from World War One. The image of Claudius hovers on the pillow next to me.

'Do you remember the third point on the path?' he says without further ado.

'Yes, it was right speech. But I fail that one almost every day. And I completely insulted the *nats* on Mount Popa in Burma.'

'It's true. But let's move on. The next is right action. Action coming from an unfettered mind. Let me give you an example. The great Muslim warrior, El-Daher-Beybars, the Sultan of Egypt and Syria in the thirteenth century, loved cats so much and was so kind and gentle to them that he devoted a garden called Gheyt-el-Quottah near his mosque to poor and unwanted cats. This is a good example of right action.'

'But I thought in real life he was terrifying and treated humans appallingly? Wasn't he known as "brave as Caesar and cruel as Nero"?'

Claudius decides to ignore this.

'I'm just trying not to believe one particular view, that's all,' I whisper sheepishly. 'Right view and all? Never mind . . .'

'The fifth point is right livelihood. Your work shouldn't do harm to others or the environment.'

But I am asleep and gently snoring.

Because it was so disgusting Dodie and I leave Phuket and fly to Hua Hin to relax at Chiva Som. Flying over Bangkok, we see traffic looping out of the city for miles in long lines of white lights like sparkling diamond necklaces.

Actually spas tend to tense me up. Part of the pampering is a boring and lengthy medical at the start of our two-day stay. We can choose from therapists who can read your cards to those who read the iris of your eye to those who read your stools. Or some such. I am unconvinced. It all feels a bit pseudo to me, but the staff are deadly serious. Of course the second I walk into a place that has no booze, limited food and yoga at seven in the morning, I want to get smashed and stoned and whoop around naked. But I take this as a sign of health. Dodie does not.

There are several people walking around with little white squares of bandage sticking to various parts of their bodies as though they're prototypes, unfinished robots, held together by bolts. This is because they have allowed some practitioner to stick tiny pins in them, which then *stay* in their skin for a few days. It's a new therapy called equilibropathy.

'Yeah, well, the lady said I was a glass blower in Dresden in the sixteenth century,' says one.

'Really?' says another. 'She told me I was an oak tree.'

'Really? And how do you feel?'

'Oh fabulous,' says the first. 'But you know, stiff.'

Surely this is just one step removed from seeing a tarot-card reader? Shouldn't you just take responsibility for your own life, regardless of the past? Yes. That's obviously the only way forward. With that realisation I tell Dodie that I can't possibly live off her any more, generous as she is. I am going to pay my own bill at Chiva Som.

'OK – whatever,' she says, her eyebrows arching.

Considering these five-star hotels charge us a fortune every time we so much as want to burp, I could be making a mistake.

Today I pull my back out doing yoga. We spend the rest of the day eating healthy fruit salads of rambutan (lychee covered in red hair like particularly spiky, scary red testicles), jackfruit (which smell and taste disgusting, though are a speciality), rose apple (deliciously fragrant, fresh, watery and green) and watermelon. The food is delicious but they ration it, so I spend most of my time fantasising about McDonald's.

We lie by a shallow green swimming pool having cold

towels pressed to our foreheads, dipping ourselves now and then in the silky water and enjoying a buffet lunch at a table decorated with melons cut into beautiful flower shapes. I then meander to the spa where I submit to a G5 vibro massage which is not unlike being put under a road-digger. Then a detoxifying body mask, that makes me sweat and sweat, is boiling and claustrophobic and not even slightly suitable, considering the heat outside.

The floors are polished dark wood, the walls are iced glass, the plunge pool is a blue surface with pink lilies, lotuses, unopened buds, leaves and flowers floating on the water, the staff are gliding silent women in uniform ready to pick up a towel touched but once and then dropped by princessy fingers. Lounging in the quiet, drinking lemon-grass cold tea, I am most concerned by a tiny, tiny frog outside the window that has spied the Jacuzzi and is dying to get into it. He cannot fathom the glass as a fly can't. He bangs against it time and time again. He yearns for the Jacuzzi and I put my finger on his image to show him he can't get through but he still doesn't click.

On our last night, we go to the night market to ogle stalls of pink and green and white sweets, fish stalls with shrimp in fish tanks and whirling fly-scarers, cheap clothes, fishermen's trousers, coconuts, bags of bright-red cherries, crowds of people, windchimes, watches, sandals, bags, hats, rainbow stripy things for hippies.

One stall has a TV blasting out the news. A story comes up of an arrested colonel. He is pulled out of a car and his clothes are ripped off. Underneath his army uniform is the bright saffron of a monk's robe. Together with the spirituality of Buddhism and the national mindset of giving exists corruption on a scale as grand as Italy's. In fact Thailand is the Italy of Southeast Asia: there is an intense love of religion, the men are exalted, the food is delicious, the people love beauty, the flowers are abundant, the corruption is inherent, the people love designer labels and children, and they love it if you try to speak the language. The one big difference of course is the temperament. The Thai temper is cool.

Back at Chiva Som we have our last healthy meal. Except it's a beach barbecue and so, freed of all restraint, we pile our plates as high as they will go, going back for fourths and fifths, so starved are we. Dancing girls are entertaining the starving troops. These lovelies are the very essence of Southeast Asian submissiveness in their gold dangling earrings, gold belts with huge bejewelled buckles, yellow straight silk skirts and black tops. With flowers in their hair they twist their long golden nails to the music, and gently gyrate, turning and lifting their hips and smiling. They're a lot lovelier than we are, that's for sure. But still I wish they wouldn't give men the impression that it's fine to hanker after submissive women.

We leave Chiva Som. In spite of the barbecue I'm still starving hungry, dying not to be touched by anyone ever again and grey at the gills from the bill.

FOURTEEN

BANGKOK TO PHIMAI TO SURIN TO BAN TA KLANG

DODIE'S TRIP IS at an end so we head back to Bangkok for one last night on the town. She wants to hit Patpong. Of course, the way we are dressed is misleading to some.

A rather old French guy with pockmarked skin asks me, 'How much?'

'Only thirty pounds from a shop across the river.'

He looks puzzled.

'You're talking about my shoes, right?'

He walks off disconsolately.

'Heh, heh, heh. Dirty old beast,' I mutter under my breath.

The streets around Patpong have a night market selling the usual eye candy: T-shirts, glittery bags, flared trousers, silk boxer shorts with elephant motifs and wooden Buddhas. Even though I have little, like a good Buddhist, I can still look. Right?

We wander into Super Pussy – a go–go bar where naked girls rub themselves up against the bar, like hungry cats wanting a home, as if to say, 'Nice man, take me away from this . . . Free me, *please*.'

A stage with half a Mustang at the back suddenly lights up. Two girls, one pigeon-toed and slim with floppy tits and the other rounder with chafing thighs, do incredible things with their fannies: they fire darts and pop balloons, they pick up flowers with chopsticks, shoot out bananas ten foot high, they write men's names with a pen, they open beer bottles, they empty the contents into themselves and then regurgitate it – yuck – and all with the most bored expressions on their faces. Finally they have sex with a dildo, chatting the entire way through.

'How's your little Sum then?'

'Oh he's fine, just back to school. Loves it.'

'Oh good, and your mum, is she better?'

'Yes thanks. How 'bout you, Tina?'

'Oh you know . . .'

Dodie has left and I feel low. A quick calculation informs me I have spent all my budget already and I still have at least a month's more travelling. I can see it'll be dirty dives from now on. I take the boat to the heart of Chinatown – a flooding Chinatown. I look for a guest house called the River View. Certainly the River View has a view of the river, from outside its very doorstep. Leaving for a stroll in the neighbourhood I wade through knee-deep brown water, with little bits of shit and whatnot skimming through my toes. Yuck. My room has a balcony and view of the river, but no bathroom and lights not strong enough to read by. From my window I can see green-tiled roofs and dragon heads, and tiny rooftops of slum dwellings with plants, and clothes hanging to dry.

In the evening there is a lovely burning apricot sunset on the river. The *sois* (small roads) around the River View Hotel have shops selling engine parts and tyres. One shop has an enormous solitary fish swimming in a green phosphorescent cloudy tank – and that's all. Every house and shop has a tiny shrine with multicoloured flashing lights and scrabby dogs lying around outside. The world's largest rat just crossed my path. My route down the *sois* takes me past a guy who is always asleep on a bench. I'm beginning to wonder whether he is alive or dead.

On Hallowe'en night I'm watching incredible fireworks explode over the river, phantom lights hanging down from the sky like skeletal pianist's hands dropping on a major chord, when the phone in my room rings.

It is Cat Cam Man! I'm incredibly excited. But unfortunately the line is bad. So he calls back. The phone rings and I pick it up but no Cat Cam Man. Instead the phone continues ringing whether I put the receiver up or down. It's like a horror film. I take the phone out of the wall to shut it up. But the second I put it back in it rings again. Eventually I lose my temper and slam the receiver down – and the phone breaks. Then as I'm taking the phone out of the room to swap it with one downstairs, the cord gets caught around the end of the bed and pulls itself out of the end – leaving just frayed wires and copper lines. It's like a scene from *Carry On Operator*. Downstairs the receptionist treats me like a criminal and assumes I have broken the phone, which er, I have. Meanwhile I'm hoping Cat Cam Man will call back but he doesn't. Argh. I'm ashamed of my temper and grateful he wasn't here to see it. My heart sinks slowly like a gold ring dropped into the Aegean Sea.

I wait a day but he doesn't call again. So I move up north because there are festivals to be seen and catteries to be visited. On the bus, the drivers and conductors are desperate for passengers as though they have shares in the company. They drive slowly and proposition anyone in a ten-mile radius of the bus, hollering the destination at them repeatedly even though the folks clearly don't want it, as though the mere repetition will make them think: Darn it! I'll go there after all!

At Phimai I check into an old shaky wooden guest house and take a motorbike taxi to the cattery in town. Sumali, the wife of the owner, has short black smooth hair and shows me several cages at the back of her roadside restaurant. There are lots of Khorat kittens, but they are all too young or too scrawny or too scared. There is a lovely Siamese male though, who is very contented in his cage with his two women whom he keeps licking. I take him out of the cage and cuddle him, but he's not that interested and keeps running away. His eyes are stunning – very light blue.

'Siamese cats used to have fiery red eyes, according to the stories. But they were turned a heavenly blue as a reward for protecting an altar from marauding barbarians.

'Blue eyes represent silver and the yellow eyes of the Burmese cat gold,' says Sumali without drawing breath. 'The possessor of both breeds of cat will always have plenty,' she smiles, picking the male Siamese up and stroking him meaningfully.

Born salesmen are the Thais. As Sumali and I discuss rabies injections in the restaurant the cat nips out the back and I wonder if we'll ever see him again. Just then he lets out a pitiful wail.

'What's happened?' I shout, worried.

'Nothing,' she laughs. 'It's the Siamese cat speaking. They're famous for it.'

This isn't the version of Cat I know.

'The story is that a particularly faithful Siamese warned the temple's guards that a thief was about to enter and they have had these loud voices ever since.'

At this point he jumps up on to her shoulder.

'Very agile too,' she adds. 'Priests believed the cats were sacred because a god had once picked one up and left the shadow of his hands for ever on its descendants – hence the markings.'

Back in town I hit Phimai's big attraction, the Khmer ruins, in order to ponder this new puss. Carved red-and-brown stone towers, untrammelled by tourists, rise against a pitch-blue sky. Partly built during the reign of Suryavarman I in the eleventh century, they face in the direction of Angkor and are situated on a former route to the old Khmer city. It is the only Khmer temple to have Buddhist themes in amongst its lintels and pediments as well as scenes from *The Ramayana*, an ancient Indian epic where good triumphs over evil.

Hiding in the cool shadows of a stone room containing

a Buddha, the walls vibrating with distant voices and lived lives, I have a peaceful backdrop for a prolonged rumination on some of life's more complicated issues: who, for instance, is higher in the food chain: humans or mosquitoes? And should I get that puss? He's the traditional Siamese cat I have been looking for. He is beautiful. Huge light-blue eyes. Huge big brown balls. But does he really like me? No, he doesn't, is the truth. I took him outside to walk around on the grass and sniff the lilac lotuses at his feet but all he wanted to do was get away from me. So I think no. Which is worrying, because Sumali's was the last cattery on Martin's checklist.

So I head off to ponder the cat dilemma at the annual elephant round-up in Surin. Surin's most famous ruler was Phraya Surin Phakdi Si Narong Wang. He became ruler of Surin province in 1760 when he helped recapture an escaped royal white elephant.

The bus careers all over the road to Surin. I see twelve elephants before I even get to my hotel. The roads are littered with poo that for once really does look like a stool. The show begins tomorrow. Late that evening I have a manicure and pedicure at a local hairdresser and watch trails of ants running all over the counters. As I pay and tip the girl for working so late, I walk into the blinds they're pulling down as they close up for the night – and create an enormous egg on my head, much to the hilarity of the manicurists, taxi drivers in the street and anyone else watching. I walk home, the sound of hoots of laughter regaling my ears.

As I wait for the lift this morning, the doors open to

reveal a woman in a black balaclava, black gloves, a gold silk jacket, a long grey skirt, black socks and pink flip-flops. She is smoking a cigarette. I get in.

'You OK?' she says.

'Fine, thank you, and you?' I reply politely, clearing my throat and keeping my eyes on the tightly shut doors.

'Yes. Where you go?'

'Elephant round-up.'

'Me too. Les go.'

She takes my arm as the doors open and clings on to me as we walk out. She moves incredibly slowly, gripping the rails of the stairs down to the lobby.

'Erm, actually I'm meeting friends,' I lie, not sure who the hell she is, or why she's gripping my arm.

'Me too. I get breakfast for my boyfriend and then we go meet my friend in hotel and go to the round-up.'

I'm not sure I like these new plans, but I hate being rude (sometimes) so I wait while she finds out the hotel doesn't do breakfast – or anything else for that matter. She guides me outside to a bicycle tuk tuk.

'OK, we go, I pay,' she says.

'The money's not the issue. What's your name?'

'Bond. James Bond.'

I smell a whiff of dry, stale alcohol.

'Listen, James.'

It feels weird calling her by a man's name but she insists. Sometimes she pronounces it Gems.

'It's *that* way,' I say as we bike off in the wrong direction.

'Just quickly see my friend,' she says.

261

We drive to the flashest hotel in town and she climbs out of the bike slowly.

'I phone my friend already – he not coming. We have a quick drink and go,' she says.

She orders herself a whisky – at 8.05 a.m. She throws her money around with the defiant anger of a drunk. At times she is polite and correct, at others she is scarily familiar, freaking out strangers. Then when they look scared, she emits angry noises.

On the way to the show she asks, 'Do you really think Princess Di is dead?'

'Er yes. I do.'

'Really? The newspapers lie to me.' She sighs. After a pause she says, 'My boyfriend, he beat me, I say OK. My father and mother beat me, I say OK. We from Buriram, very poor farmers, rice growers. My sister I love.' Then seconds later she says, 'I give her 100,000 baht just to get her the fuck out of my face.'

'What?'

'I go to work in Bangkok sometimes. I dance and then when I sleep with men the guy he takes all the money, 300 baht.' (About a fiver.) 'Nothing for me. I hate boys.'

'Are you a prostitute?' I ask, all tact, making for the nearest exit.

'No. I'm not prostitute. When I sleep with men I don't always ask them for money. They want to fuck to touch you all over and hurt you. I don't like it.'

She spits the words out.

'How long have you been drinking?'

'Since I was seventeen. I'm thirty-six now.'

'But your English is so good. You could work in the travel industry or something. Why don't you get yourself out of this pickle? Why rely on men to support you when you could do it yourself and feel good about yourself?'

She leans over and breathes whisky all over me.

'I have film-star name,' she whispers. 'But I don't live in California.'

Right then.

At the round-up I make the mistake of buying 30-baht seats, refusing to pay the 500 baht – the fleeced *farang* price. Instead I am surrounded by Thais craning over each other to see the show; I am unable to see anything or hear any of the American commentary provided for the expensive seats. Little boys in *Easy Rider of Ontario* T-shirts and I pile on to an ice cooler, which we have to budge from every five minutes when the woman selling scary-looking red-and-green drinks needs to scoop ice out of it.

The nelly show takes ages and ages because they lumber around quite a lot. Finally I squeeze backstage, where warriors in red sarongs tied up between their legs, with bare chests and arms and legs and red ties around their heads, smoke and chat, where nellies dressed in beautiful purple and burgundy and gold warrior costumes eye me with their softly long eyelashes and wrinkled eyes and sniff around me for bananas.

What do the elephants do? They pot balls into basketball nets, they dance, they stand on three legs, they hold each other's tails, they run a bit, they step over men. The warriors charge each other in a rerun of the victory of King Naresuan (1590–1605) who attacked the Burmese on elephant-back. James sits on the floor with her beer and misses all of this. Not surprisingly she's not interested.

Finally a synchronised dance by brightly made-up boys and girls with flowers in their hair, in blue and yellow and pink silk tops, curling their hands and wrists prettily. Later the nellies play football with an oversized ball and some of them cheat by picking it up with their trunks and running to the goal with it, which just shows how intelligent they are. Then a tug of war and it is very satisfying watching one elephant pull over sixty men as though they are skittles.

Gems and I walk back.

'I introduce you to my boyfriend. You say hello to him,' she says.

I feel she's about to turn pimp.

'No thanks, Gems, I'm really not interested.'

By this stage she is very, very drunk.

'Let me lie down, I feel ill,' she says.

'Which is your room?'

'Oh no, don't make me lie with him. I want to rest.'

Feeling slightly reluctant, I take her to my room.

'Have one drink with me,' she says, having bought a whisky bottle on the way. I suppose I could relax my anti-drinking stance, considering she's a woman and not likely to draw any conclusions about me being a bad Buddhist.

Four hours later I wake up groggy and wondering where the hell I am. Slowly memories of James resurface to my pool of consciousness. Looking round, I see my room is a tip – I have been raided. I make for my bag – which is free of any money, credit cards or aeroplane tickets. Gems can't have been that drunk. She knew what she was looking for all right. I can't understand how two sips of whisky can produce this throbbing head – unless it was drugged. I want to cry – but feel all dried up inside.

A desperate chat with reception reveals there was never anyone of that description staying in the hotel. By some miracle they don't remember seeing me with her or even me getting my key from them before we went up. The whole thing is useless. I present myself to the local police, who are in a party mood because of the festival, and couldn't care less. I then cancel my credit cards and get more money.

After the most stressful afternoon in history, I make my way back to the hotel and stroke a random elephant's nose for comfort. The mahout is young and beady-eyed.

'You OK?'

This was James's opening gambit, so I'm not keen on repeating the experience.

'No. Not at all.'

'Why?'

I pour the story out and add a few cat insecurities for good measure. I'm not that interested in slowing down to make my English more comprehensible, I just figure he'll have to keep up and I need a good moan.

'You need to relax,' he laughs.

Why do Thais always laugh when people are upset? It winds me up even more.

'Look at this beautiful place. Look at my beautiful elephant. Have a ride. Special Plice.'

'He's lovely,' I sniff desolately. 'What's his name?'

'Moomba.'

He helps me up and it is definitely relaxing to move at a slower pace and see the world from another viewpoint.

'Where did you get your elephant?' I ask as we mosey down streets. I feel rather conspicuous and headachey under the sun.

'I take him from wild.'

He accompanies 'wild' by a great rolling of the eyes and baring of the teeth and growling noise which are somewhat unsettling and frankly unnecessary.

'We hunt him.'

'Who?'

'Me and other mahouts.'

'Really? Can I be a mahout too?'

'Oh no. Women forbidden to touch tools and ropes needed or they break the magic.'

'Oh baloney.'

'Oh what?'

'Oh baloney. Where are you from?'

'Ban Ta Klang. Little village sixty kilometres from here. Many elephants.'

'And you think women can't be mahouts?'

'That's right.'

'Well, I'll see you in Ban Ta Klang. And I'll show you the bond that exists between women and elephants.'

'OK, my friend,' he smiles. 'Time up. Get off.'

And as soon as I can, I up and off to Ban Ta Klang.

Ban Ta Klang is in a rejoicing mood at this time of year after the Surin celebrations. It is a village made up almost entirely of elephants and their mahouts, or so it seems. The morning after my arrival, I wake very early just as the sun is coming up. I potter quietly out of my guest house and down to the elephant corral to see what's up. A couple of mahouts smile at me. They're leading the elephants down to the lake. The elephants mosey after them. Some younger over-excited ones run ahead. They wallop into the lake. Elephant after elephant lumbers into the water. It must be very deep in certain places as some elephants disappear completely but for their trunks sticking up like wrinkly slate periscopes. My heart is rising.

The mahouts scrub the nearest elephants, their loose blue clothes soaking up water as the job gets more vigorous. They beckon to me to join in. It's quite chilly, but one small elephant leads me further into the water, in my trousers and shirt. Soon I'm swimming with the elephants. We go further and further into the lake. A huge body moves below – an elephant deep in the water swimming under me. Incredible. How do they keep all that weight buoyant? Or maybe it is ambling along the bottom of the lake. Just as I'm musing on this, that elephant does an underwater somersault in the green and muddy water. My breath catches sharp with the cool of the water and the sight of a huge somersaulting elephant. Then the elephant rises from the depths, like Poseidon, and rolls me on to its back and surfaces like a

267

submarine. It swims off and three others follow us squirting water from their trunks.

When the mahouts call, the elephants near the bank climb out. My younger friends and I are still playing, but they carry me out of the lake into the morning. For the first time in years I feel settled in my own skin. Afterwards I want to share it with someone, but there isn't an English speaker in sight. I toy with the idea of phoning Cat Cam Man but feel an opening gambit of 'I'm swimming with elephants. How are you?' might seem a little strange, so chicken out.

After a couple more days like this the elephants begin to know me. When I go into the corral, they move aside a little, just enough to let me through, and by instinct know when to move back so that a Mexican wave of elephant creates a path. It is wondrous, and yet still slightly scary.

One morning I am having my breakfast of a banana pancake, when a baby elephant comes into the kitchen and messes around under the table. It jogs the table and lifts it on to its back so that my food shifts from me like a phantom magic carpet of wheat and banana. This is fun for a while but just as I'm starting to get bored with following my breakfast around the room, the baby stops as though it's psychic. Of course I'm now entertaining fantasies of having a baby elephant instead of a cat.

FIFTEEN

SUKHOTHAI

FEELING MUCH HAPPIER, I move on to Sukhothai, a place of great historic interest. It was the first capital of the Thai people, and was at its most powerful in the thirteenth century under the rule of King Ramkamhaeng, who modified the Sri Lankan script to create the Thai alphabet. But more importantly it is the best place to celebrate Loy Krathong, a festival that pays homage to the goddess of waterways and rivers, Mae Khongkha.

A few hours' bus ride away past rice fields and trees with branches dropping big yellow blossom is the historic town of Sukhothai. I'm dropped in the blazing sun I have no idea where, but I get a motorised cart, a very strange contraption, a bike that has put the cart before the horse, so to speak, which does a tour of the local guest houses. Searching for the 99 guest house, I'm told by other proprietors (including the sister of the owner of 99 herself, I later realise), that it no longer exists.

But I eventually find it. It is wooden from top to bottom with lovely big rooms with a fan and large double bed. The downside is that there are two insane dogs across the road – one is rabid and the other whines continually all through the night. Na, the owner, speaks good English and is incredibly helpful. She immediately tells me the secret of eternal youth (melon every day) but doesn't like to go into more detail than 'hydrates' on this issue. She looks very young with perfect line-free skin, even though she's hitting forty.

The heat here beats all other furnace-like places hitherto experienced. The new city lies twelve kilometres east of the old city, near the river. The old city is an historical park. I cycle round it, which, considering the heat, is a quite extraordinarily stupid idea. It doesn't occur to me to check the brakes when I hire my bike, and as I careen into one of the city's loveliest old buildings to the tuts of all onlookers, I curse that woman who promised me the cheapest ride in town. I might have given myself a dose of sunstroke but the *wats* are lovely crumbly old things.

The ruins, in old Khmer style – as Sukhothai used to be an outpost of the Khmer kingdom – are impressive. They include old Khmer *prangs*, often three in a row: brick, zeppelin-shaped objects pointing up to the sky, that symbolise Mount Meru, the mythical home of the gods, and are intricately carved with *nagas* – multi-headed serpents for protection against evil spirits – and Hindu and Buddhist deities. Around these ruins, in the early thirteenth century, King Si Intharathit built *bots* (eastern-facing halls for monks) and *wihans* (larger halls) to house Buddha images. He also added brick multi-layered *chedis*, which were based on Sri Lankan bell-shaped reliquaries. Other *chedis* have lotus buds at their apex. The deserted ruins are sprinkled with grass growing between steps as thin as paper or as fat as loaves of bread. Stone friezes of monks walking to oblivion have started to erode, and nearby ponds choke with dawdling lotus flowers.

I wander to the nearby King Ramkamhaeng Monument.

'Do you know what King Ramkamhaeng handed down to us?'

I jump with alarm at the sight of Claudius, who has appeared with a bang and is now sitting in a blur of brown haze on top of the monument.

'No idea, Claude.'

'Shall I tell you? White elephants! He decided that white elephants were prestigious – and that the more a king had the more powerful he was. You realise, I presume, that white elephants are of such importance because Queen Maya dreamt of one before giving birth to the Buddha? Do you know what expression they inspired?'

'Er, "a white elephant", perhaps?'

Does he really think I'm that thick?

'Meaning a large useless object, because being royal the elephants weren't allowed to work. It was very expensive to keep them in luxury. So prestigious were they that when young they were suckled by women.'

'Oh *yuck*.'

'It's true. It was an honour for women to suckle such a great beast and so loads of women were prepared to do it. They are a good example of the sixth point on the path to enlightenment: right effort. The seventh is right mindfulness – not forgetting the real source of our problems, suffering. And the eighth is right concentration, i.e. keeping your mind focused and aware.'

And with that he is gorn in a puff of furry brown smoke.

Just then a girl comes running up.

'Are you OK?'

'Of course, yes. Why?'

'Because you've been standing there whispering into thin air. You feel OK? Sure?'

At the end of the day, I meander around the new city looking for I don't know what. I come across just that – a *wat*. I'm walking through the grounds – it's rather late, and very dark. I'm at a particularly black and unlit point when I wonder if perhaps I might get mugged – a Londoner to the end. Should I turn back? My feet make a hesitatory movement, but *no*, don't be scared, I think, and with the next step something small moves ahead of me. Its movement is too springy for a rat although it's the right size. Looking closer I see it's a kitten. In fact, I'm surrounded by kittens. Once they realise I'm friendly they scamper around me. The closest building is a small temple. Just outside is a cage with the most lovely pair of kittens inside – they look like Khorats.

'Hello!' squeaks one.

'Hello!' squeaks the other.

'Hello!' says the first.

'Hello!' squeaks the other.

'Shush, I'm saying hello for us,' says the first, stepping in front of the other.

'Aren't you beautiful?' I say, letting them out of the cage and stroking them.

Luckily they don't hop it for the nearest tree but purr strongly and climb all over my legs and arms.

'You speak *Cat*!' shouts the second, sniffing my fingers, one ear slightly back, his nose twitching.

'Well, I suppose we are rather lovely,' says the first, sitting down and puffing out his chest proudly.

He blink-smiles, turns his head to the side and tries not to look too pleased.

'What are your names?'

'Um, um, our names are —'

'We don't have them!' squeaks the second, pouncing on the tail of the first.

'Hmm. How about Loy and Krathong?'

'Why?' they ask simultaneously.

'After the festival in a couple of days' time.'

'So we're Loy and Krathong?' says Loy.

'We're Khorats!' says Krathong apropos of nothing. 'We're *lucky*!' he says importantly.

'We're given as wedding presents usually,' says Loy, moving closer so that Krathong's advances on to my lap are curtailed.

After a pause, I say, 'I'd love to take you two out of this cage for good and away . . .'

'*Oh!*'

Loy tries not to look excited.

'Where to?'

'London.'

'*Oh.*'

'Where?' squeaks Krathong.

'Lumbum,' says Loy authoritatively.

'Where's that?'

'Shush. Would we be in this cage?'

'No.'

'Do you have the wide-open?'

'Well, I have a big terrace and it leads to lots of others.'

'*Oh! Oh!*'

Loy bounds around a bit, purring.

'Ow! You're on my tail,' shouts Krathong.

Although silver in colour, these twin brothers are miniature Claudiuses. Full of strength, they push their soft coats back against my strokes, they purr loudly, climb over me, explore the grounds – they are clearly very rarely let out of the cage. And if I had turned back when I was scared – I'm thrilled to bits. As the woman in *When Harry Met Sally* says of meeting the right man, 'You know the way you know a good melon.' I feel the same. I've found what I'm looking for – my cats. They are The Ones. I just *know*.

As they explore, an emaciated old monk approaches from behind the Buddha statues. He gets out sausage to feed the cats. At last, someone who knows cats must eat protein and not rice, but the cats fight for the meat – it's not a pretty sight. They could have each other's eyes out.

I love the way cats never resent each other after a spat. After growling and scratching, everything goes back to normal. The monk is very fair and gives the cats several bits of sausage each.

I ask the monk about the cats but he is more concerned about giving me a bag of tangerines and apples and biscuits and a pomegranate. Surely I should be giving to him rather than the other way round.

'Take them! Take them!' whispers Loy.

'Why? I should be offering to him!'

'Because it's a national holiday today. The Phra Piya Maharaj died this day, the 23rd of October, 1910.'

'The who?'

'The king who loved cats! Chulalongkorn. It is Chulalongkorn Day!'

I take this as an immensely good sign. So I receive the gift happily and make a donation to the golden Buddha images. Sometimes the gold leaf isn't smooth; it flutters in the breeze like broken skin – the Buddhas look, somewhat unsettlingly, like corpses.

I try not to kill too many mosquitoes in the monk's presence – as a result I'm bitten to death. Our communication is limited to many guttural Thai noises on his side and 'England, I love cats' on mine. Better to return with a Thai speaker, I decide. I turn to tell the kittens this but they are otherwise occupied.

'He's biting me.'

'I'm not.'

'He's biting me.'

'He's not,' I say, because looking at Krathong I can see he's not.

'He did, though.'

'When?'

Loy pauses and looks away with dignity.

'Yesterday,' he sniffs.

'Right. Right.'

He sniffs again and looks fascinated by a picture on the wall of the temple.

I put the kittens back in their cage.

'Now be good and I'll be back tomorrow,' I whisper.

They settle down to sleep curled inside each other, like racing tracks.

Excited, I make my way back to Na, who agrees to be my translator, once she has described the hill tribes she helps, and talked a lot about tips and not taking them herself but giving them to the poor. I get the gist and promise to make a donation to the hill tribes in return, which seems fair enough.

Next day Na and I go to the temple to speak with the monk.

'Take the best fruit,' says Na. 'The monk is just below the king in our social hierarchy, so give him the best.'

We bow and scrape our way into the temple to speak with him. When the kittens see us they stretch and paw at the cage.

'Are you two cremated?' Krathong asks, yawning and waving his paw to indicate Na and me.

'Er no, not yet,' I whisper.

'Who is she then?'

'She's here to help us. Where's the monk?'

They both look towards a statue, from behind which the monk is watching us carefully. When he sees he has been seen, he gets out food for the cats, and Na explains my predicament. They speak for some time, while I give more donations to the Buddha and chat with the kittens. Na asks me some questions, where I'll take them, when, how, etc.

'He says he can see you, like him, love cats. But he is not yet sure, because he gave some cats away once before and they died.'

'Please assure him I'll treat them like kings. That will never happen with me.'

She speaks to him. She turns back to me.

'He says to return after Loy Krathong and he will have decided.'

Not the answer I was hoping for, but he seems friendly enough and Loy Krathong is only the day after tomorrow. I return to the guest house cursing the dogs and blessing the moon.

Today it is hotter than ever – I feel sunstrokey after five minutes in the sun. I hope the monk will say yes. I can't really imagine him saying no. Wouldn't it be against every tenet of his religion? And 'no' is a word not known in Cat.

The other guests in Na's house include a couple of Irish and two Dutch girls. We're off to celebrate Loy Krathong.

Before we leave, we hide our valuables carefully. I have a money belt on me, but it is chock-a-block with passport and money and there is simply no room for the gem I bought in Mae Sot. I have no desire to leave it in the house, which is unlocked. Everyone is at the festival and, convinced that this is the time for burglars to get their best pickings, I keep the girls waiting deciding what to do.

'An idea,' say the Irish girls. 'Why don't you swallow that gem if you don't want to put it in your pocket?'

'What?'

'Swallow it. It'll come out in a couple of days, good as new.'

'OK. It's a *great* idea!'

And I pop it in my mouth. And swallow. Urgh.

'Of course you should have washed it first,' they say. 'You never know where your hands have been.'

In a large girl posse we make for the old city on roads blocked for miles. I feel slightly queasy. The petrol fumes choke us. But the ruins are breathtaking. Every *chedi*, every *wat*, every *bot* has been covered in candles, and with people wandering around and over them they have come to life. They are breathing with the festival. Stalls line every pathway. The place mills with thousands of people; some lie asleep on the grass on sheets of wrapping paper. Loud speakers announce events, and blare music.

The Sound and Light show at Wat Mahathat has a cast of thousands and full fireworks at the end. Being in Thai it's all Greek to me. The story is obviously the history of Sukhothai, with kings and wars and beautiful princesses and all being explained by an old man to a young girl. The man behind me has brought his poodles to the show. That'll be me tomorrow with the kittens. They let candlelit lanterns off that amble slowly up against the black sky, like golden Nefertiti heads floating up to the heavens. When I let off my own later, it resembles my life – at first it refuses to take off then suddenly it sways up and wobbles ferociously on some terrifying axis, this way and that, until it is carried off on a stream higher and higher and becomes totally uncontrollable. Now and then bits of the burning candle shoot back down to earth.

Enormous competition *krathongs* line the ponds, all lit up. They are colourful displays of carving containing lanterns made from dried rice, and wooden houses and dragons and tiny figures intricately made. Little *krathongs* made of flowers and banana leaves with a candle and incense stick in the middle are for sale for 20 baht. We buy one, drop a hair and piece of nail into the centre, then float it while making a wish. Guess what I wish for.

Stalls selling silks, fabrics and sarongs. Stalls selling meat kebabs, balls of chicken, shrimp, baked eggs, corn on the cob, *phad thai*, sweets, Coke and lemonade, beer, cigarettes, camera film, plastic masks for children. Stalls selling fried creepy-crawlies: worms, slugs, locusts, and cicadas. Dodgy playground rides. Dodgem cars and a ghost house the size of a tent and a small very unstable big wheel.

Everyone is in a couple – even the Irish girls. It seems I am the only single person on this planet. When we can stand the crowds no longer we head back to the guest house where we all tiptoe to bed. I must sleep well and be all fresh for tomorrow (Monk Day) but I sleep rather lightly because all the couples in the house are trying to have quiet sex, the combined efforts of which are making the wooden house shake.

The day of reckoning. Incredibly jittery and excited, I go to see the monk with copious amounts of juicily coloured fruit for him. He is rather more Zen than me. In fact he is so Zen, he expresses nothing, and I wonder if he remembers why I'm here. But the Khorats are pleased to see me. One has a gooey eye and for a second I think something hideous has happened, that the eye has been taken out by another cat – but it's just goo. I let them wander around and cuddle them and one even sits on my lap of his own accord. What other evidence can the monk need to see we're meant for each other?

Na translates.

'He says you and he are the same. You love cats. But if he gives you them he will be alone.'

'But he has all these other cats!'

'But these are his favourite too.'

'Isn't he meant not to be attached to material things?'

She doesn't reply.

'He says there is another girl who wants one. If he gives one to you she will be sad, and if he gives one to her you will be sad and if he gives you one each he will be sad.'

'Can't he accept the sadness as part of his karma? No?

OK, forget I said it. Actually I think it's very important the kittens stay together. I would hate them to be separated.'

I can't quite believe I said that.

'This other girl helps him with transportation some-times. What can you do for him, he is asking?'

'Er, I don't know. Anything he wants?'

'He says he would be willing to part with the kittens in exchange for a car.'

'You're kidding, right?'

Just then a light bulb appears above my head.

'I have a jewel! A ruby from Mae Sot. It cost a fortune.'

She speaks to him.

'OK. He is interested. Where is it?'

'Ah, well, you see, I'll have to get it from the guest house.'

'Fine. Shall we wait for you here?'

'Oh, er, it may take a day or so.'

'He says bring it as soon as you can.'

With that we up and off.

'Where are you going? What's happening?' squeak the kittens in unison.

'I have to give something in exchange for you, and I don't have it on me. Well, to be precise, I have it *in* me, but I have to get hold of it more literally, shall we say?'

The kittens look wide-eyed and confused. Then again this might just be because they're cats.

Back at Na's place, I wander up and down wringing my hands.

'What's wrong?' asks Na.

'I need to, um,' I say. 'How can I make things move along? Prunes! Do you have any?'

'Prunes? What are they?'

'They're a fruit.'

'No. Melon? Do you want some melon?'

'No, I need something that will get me, er, moving.'

I make a round-and-round patacake gesture on my tummy.

'Oh . . .' she says. 'I'll get my cook to organise something for you.'

Half an hour later she comes up with a foul-smelling liquid that she forces me to drink. Sure enough a few hours later I'm on the run. Literally. I make a pact not to eat anything more, so as not to confuse my system and to get everything out of there as quickly as possible.

Next morning she gives me more. By this stage things are moving so freely and so often I can't believe I haven't yet heard the clunk of gem on porcelain. But I haven't. Two days later I am a) starving and b) convinced that something horrid has happened.

'Are you sure you haven't already, you know, dropped it?' she asks.

'No, I'm absolutely sure. For a start I look and secondly I'd hear it and thirdly there's no food left in me any more anyway.'

'Maybe it's just floating around in your system like a lost planet, and eventually its edges will be worn down until they rip through your –'

'Yes, thank you, Na, that's a lovely thought. But I don't think it can be floating around. Though it's certainly not out yet either. I don't know what to do.'

A day later I can no longer wait.

'Na, I have to go and talk to him. I don't want that other girl to get those kittens.'

'What about the jewel?'

'The jewel is a complete mystery. I think I can feel it inside me, I'm not sure, but it is clearly not coming out. I'll just have to offer him money.'

We head for the temple again. He does not look pleased by my lack of jewel. I get out a wad of cash instead.

'Put it on the floor. He cannot take it directly from your hand,' says Na.

I do so. He picks up the money and studies it closely. He puts it back on the floor and talks to Na.

'He says that he gave some cats away before and they were treated badly.'

'Oh *Na*! Not that again. If only he *knew*. I'll treat those kittens like demi-gods. They'll have the best life imaginable. Much better than the life here where they're continually cooped up in a cage.'

They talk for a long time.

'What is he saying?'

'He says the same thing over and over. He is difficult to understand because he stutters so much. He can't say no because that is a sin but the way he is wording it, it is not yes either. And, Clare, if I continue harassing him, that is a sin for me too.'

I can't believe it. Without saying no, he has said no. He's skeletal and I can't help feeling he's going to die soon *anyway* and then what'll happen to the cats? I turn to the kittens.

'When are we going then?' squeals Loy, chasing his tail and walloping himself around the cage.

'Are we going now?' sings Krathong.

'No,' I reply quietly. 'The monk doesn't want to part with you.'

'Why not?' whispers Loy.

'Because you're so lovely.'

My eyes well up.

'Are we staying in this cage then?' says Loy, his eyes very wide.

'Yes, it looks like it. For the time being anyway.'

They both flump down disconsolately. And I have to walk away.

Now I feel a failure. I suppose I could buy any old pedigree cat out here but I don't want just any old cat. I want Loy and Krathong. We're meant for each other. I don't know what to do now.

I am in bed thinking when suddenly a rich smell of frankincense, candles, champagne and all things lovely fills the air. Sure enough Claudius is materialising at the end of the bed. His darling whiskery face has a 'Well well well' look on it. I sob at the sight of him. I want to cuddle him.

'Well, chum, you look about as happy as a Khorat in a rain ceremony,' he says.

'What's that?' I sniffle.

'It's an ancient rain-making ceremony from the rural areas of Thailand. During times of drought, Thais used to parade a Khorat cat (a dry animal) from morning to night in a wicker cage through the village. Water was thrown on the cage until the animal was drenched – as a means of lifting the curse of the drought.'

'The cat can't have enjoyed it much.'

'No. That's why I liken your face to it.'

'Oh Claude. He said *no*.'

'Of course he said no. Now then, there's only one way to look at this . . .'

'Please don't tell me there's some lesson in here.'

'You did say you wanted to be a Buddhist. Acceptance . . .'

'Really? Is that what I said? Well, let me rephrase it. If I have a choice between having those kittens and being a good Buddhist, I choose the kittens.'

'Ahh, well, that's a retrospective wish. You asked for the Buddhism before the kittens.'

'Oh Claude, you're breaking my heart.'

I sob quietly, he purrs loudly. He always does this when I cry. I think it's meant to comfort. But it has the same effect as the Thais laughing, even when I've had a tuk tuk accident.

'And the jewel?' he purrs.

'Er, I have no idea.'

'Now listen,' he continues. 'It's not such a bad thing not having another cat.' In fact he looks quite pleased by the idea. 'Think of Thomas Hardy. He loved his cat so much that when it died he refused to have another.'

'But I thought he did have another eventually.'

'Well, yes, he did. A Persian, a very silly fluffy breed, I might say. But remember Hardy's words: *Never another pet for me. Let your place all vacant be!*'

The next evening I return. The monk's body language is unmistakable. He has no desire to see me. He raises his arm from the elbow up and down and then turns swiftly round in a couple of circles. Actually he looks as though he is performing the Thai version of 'The Birdie Song'. I'm about to join him, except he walks off in the opposite direction. He then hides behind a tree until I leave. It's a gesture of 'Be gone with you!' And who can blame him – some silly *farang* girl not giving him peace.

Another monk offers to find me some kittens, but they won't be these Khorats and it's like after being chucked when your girlfriend says, 'Come out and meet my friend – he's a great guy.' It's too soon and you know it won't be the same. My life feels as difficult and tangled as coarsened hair that's been windkissed in a convertible. I need reverse therapy. Something bigger and better: tigers, for instance. I'll go hiking in Khao Yai forest, where there are fifty of them.

SIXTEEN

KHAO YAI TO KHORAT
TO LONDON

TODAY I MAKE my way, kittenless, to Pak Chang, the nearest town to Khao Yai National Forest. This involves an eight-hour bus ride through Western-style towns and unpavemented wide dusty roads with low buildings that look unfinished, and one main highway. The bus has thirty people crammed down the central aisle. They stand like that for six hours, which means the loo is inaccessible. Murder. A woman with a sticky, greasy-haired little girl on her lap sits next to me. She lets her child loll all over me. The Thais adore children but having been denied my kittens, I'm not feeling that maternal.

Once in Khorat I take another bus for an hour and a half to Pak Chang. The bus (decorated with a picture of five toothless and decrepit monks, their mouths collapsing in on themselves, their skinny legs in the lotus position, their bodies floating above each other like members of a boy band in a poster) passes petrol stations ironically called Lemon Green as though they were pure and fresh. Now I'm absolutely bus-ridden and sore to death. The problem with these buses is you have no idea which stop to get off at.

At Pak Chang's night market I eat a delicious supper of tiny soft shell crabs in a lime, sugar, mint and soya sauce. Next day I get up early, breakfast (noodles squirming around tastelessly) and take a bus to the national park, all ready for my tiger expedition. It's the usual thing – I'm not sure whether the bus is going in the right direction or when to get off, but I just sit there happily enough. I then hitch-hike with a bunch of Swedes in a battered white pickup truck to the National Forest headquarters.

Near the headquarters the car stops so we can take pictures of gibbons on the road. I turn round to get my camera and the guy opposite me is more interested in what's on his leg – an enormous insect – black and orange with a thick body, like a wasp, but about twenty times the size. I'm about to take a picture when the insect flies up into my hair. I try to brush the creature off, but it won't go. I panic more and more until I'm flailing and shouting, 'Get it off me! Get it off me!' Then the bastard stings me. Finally it flies off. None of the Swedes help – perhaps they didn't want to touch the thing. I shake, in shock, and my head throbs in agony. I want to cry and a few tears roll down. We drive on. I feel miserable.

Eventually a girl asks me how I feel.

'I'm worried in case poison has been injected into my brain,' I whimper.

'Yes, I'd worry about that too if I were you,' she says helpfully.

Her boyfriend sort of kicks her leg and says, 'Yes, it's OK. It happen to me two years back and pain went away after half an hour. You OK.'

I find this more comforting (though three hours later am wondering when the pain will go).

At the park I find a guide. I have no idea whether I'm going to die or not. But I go trekking anyway. Even though I'm in flip-flops. Yes, for some reason I have flip-flops on. And even though I hate trekking, a fact I always forget. Like the pain of childbirth. Not that I've ever given birth.

Throughout the trek my head throbs non stop and I wonder if I'm doing the sensible thing or whether I should check myself straight into hospital. I'm in a cold sweat the entire time. I'm convinced my hair will fall out, I'll be in a coma for days, my teeth will drop out, my scalp rot – everything.

Finally at the observation watch tower – we see nothing. But I do manage to slip down the stairs, jarring my back very painfully when I land with a thump on my bum. By this stage I'm in agony, and could really do with the reward of seeing a tiger. But instead my guide points out a very long worm and some 'why dock cheet' (wild dog shit). Not even that's fresh. It's been there for days.

'Why don't you camp here?' suggests the guide.

'Oh please,' I reply. 'Don't be ridiculous. I'm not the campy kinda girl and I don't want to star in any more Thai versions of *The Day of the Triffids*.'

I hate nature.

I down some *namanao*, a cracking lime-and-sugar drink, with green pills, green for primeval goo, evil, toxin. These are the pills the doctor (who seems to think I'll live but I'm not so sure) has just given me to get rid of the evil swirling around in my head. The sac of poison has moved from my head down to my cheek. Under my skin is a pocket of liquid like a waterbed. I estimate time of arrival at my heart being midday tomorrow sometime. I take to my bed for a think.

How can I rid myself of my loneliness? Can't I be like the fox that bites off its leg to remove the pain of the trap? What part of myself do I have to lose to escape? I am completely catless. A feline-free zone. Perhaps I could have one final crack at it in Khorat. There are bound to be cats there. It's where the Sukhothai kittens came from, after all.

I'm in a dingy, unfriendly guest house miles away from the centre of Khorat: the Doctor Guess House. I think their amusing word play is unintentional but considering the patriarch *is* a doctor, I find it worrying, and decide not to consult him re my increasingly aching back. Nor do I tell him about my bed, which this morning was covered in mouse droppings.

Not knowing what else to do, I wander around Khorat like a lost sheep. Maybe I'll just go to the mall and content myself with Western surroundings. But once there, a strange sense of lethargy comes over me. I don't feel quite alive. It's as if there's no happy balance between the frustration of Southeast Asia and the soulless sop of shopping. I hit the e-mail shop, looking for signs of life from Cat Cam Man. A girl named Mo approaches me. She has been offered a job by a guy in Bangkok offering little money and wants help penning a letter asking for more, which I'm happy to do. In return she takes me to the town's one note of interest, the Thao Suranari monument.

'I am named after her!' she says proudly. 'Her name is Khunying Mo.'

In 1826, when under attack from Prince Anuwong of Vientiane, Khorat was saved by Khunying Mo, whose husband, the deputy governor, was away on business. With some chums she fed the invading soldiers alcohol and then killed them as they enjoyed a hungover snooze. The monument has her standing with her hand jauntily on her hip. We offer some flowers to her in the hope that we will be as cool in the face of problematic men.

Mo herself is a real fighter. She helps support her parents.

'My father is a builder but he hasn't worked in five years. My mother is angry with him and nags him a lot, so he often goes to stay with his second wife.'

'Does he have children with her?'

'Yes, an entire second family.'

'What about you? Are you married?'

'No. My sister is getting married tomorrow but I'm single. I split up from my boyfriend two months ago.'

'I'm so sorry.'

'Yes, he was two-timing me with a Japanese girl. I

loved him but I knew it wasn't right. So I prefer to be alone.'

'What do you want, Mo?'

'Money. So I can study. So I can learn to swim. So I can set up a beauty business.'

She takes me to the night market hoping there might be cats there. There's the usual bunch of cheap tat and puppies in cages, terrapins and gerbils, but nothing else. At the end of the evening we check our e-mail and Mo has been given a pay rise by her future employer. She is so excited that to thank me she invites me to her sister's wedding the next day.

'I'd love to come but are you sure that's OK?' I reply.

I can think of nothing nicer than spending the day at a proper Thai event.

'I will talk with my parents and come and find you tomorrow morning.'

Which she does. At seven o'clock. I bolt up groggily, dress in my best clothes, which are not half good enough for a wedding, slap some slap on my face quickly and head off with her in a tuk tuk. She has purple orchids in her hair and wears lots of bright make-up and looks lovely.

'Your ex-boyfriend was very silly, Mo,' I say.

'Thank you,' she smiles. 'I hope today is a good day. The astrologers told my sister she should marry today.'

'Why?'

'It's an even-numbered month. We believe that these are auspicious for weddings because there are two people in a marriage and so the month must be a multiple of two.'

We arrive at her parents' compound. It is not big and they are not rich people and this is immediately evident.

'If your father hasn't worked for five years . . . ?' I start.

'The bridegroom pays,' she replies quietly.

'Excellent.'

'Yes. Probably because he's so grateful not to be a *khon kaeng* any more.'

'What's that?'

'It means an unfinished man. After monkhood men try and get married pretty quickly because, if they don't, people gossip and think there must be something wrong with them because no one has entrusted their daughters to them.'

'Really?'

This is such exciting news in the war of the sexes.

'Well, sort of. Not so much nowadays, to be honest.'

'Oh.'

Still.

I follow her out of the tuk tuk into the house, which is small but very clean. The main room has eight monks sitting in a semicircle. Mo's sister and her fiancé are seated within the semicircle. Her sister has her hair up in an intricate, pearl-beaded style. She has beautiful make-up and a simple lilac dress with sequins and beads decorating the hems and collar. The fiancé is in a dark suit. They are both holding incense. We sit at the back quietly.

'What have they got on their heads?' I whisper to Mo.

'*Mongkuls* – crowns which symbolise unity,' she whispers back.

The monks are holding a thin white thread, which was bound round an altar to the Buddha, and held by each of the monks. It then passed out of the window all the way round the house and back through another window to the altar to be held by the first monk of the row.

'What's the white thread for?' I whisper again.

'It protects everyone inside it,' whispers Mo back. 'It's called the *sai sin*. It's a sacred cord.'

The monks chant. The head monk says a blessing. They lull us almost to sleep, so beautiful and calming are the completely incomprehensible words. After this they roll back the sacred cord and the head monk sprinkles sacred water on the couple and on the rest of us. We then pour out into the sun and cross the compound where we are served fantastic food – after the monks have been served, of course – bowl upon bowl of steaming rice with succulent meats running in blood-coloured juicy sauces, and fried vegetables, and multicoloured sweet puddings. Afterwards the bride and groom head a procession out of the dining room, and two guys carrying bamboo branches form an arch over the couple as they walk.

Mo and I rest afterwards and hang around talking. Her family are very accommodating and she translates between us. Later in the afternoon, about four o'clock, we go to the main ceremony to which the couple's friends have been invited. This is in a large hall down the road, because it is a much bigger occasion.

'It is called *rot nam*,' explains Mo. 'It is water-pouring.'

Dreading something along the lines of Thingyan, I am relieved to see that the water-pouring involves a small amount poured from a conch shell on to the couple's hands. The room is heaving with people and chatter; they stand in a long line according to rank and age. As usual all the men are first.

'It's in remembrance of the times when men went off to battle and the women stayed home to look after the house,' explains Mo. 'We have an old saying that in a marriage men are the fore legs and women the hind legs of an elephant. They help each other but they must be in the proper place in accordance with their characteristics.'

'And what do you think of that?' I ask.

'Not a lot,' she replies, and we smile.

The bride and groom are squatting on a low bench with their hands in the prayer/*wai* position. The bride is on the groom's left-hand side. Their two crowns have now been bound together with a cord. Flower garlands adorn their necks.

Mo is far ahead of me in the line by this stage because she is family, and I am pretty much last, which is fitting. I feel a bit nervous because I have no idea what to say. I watch everyone ahead of me anxiously and when it is my turn I take the pretty conch shell from the head guest and tip a torrent of water over the bride's tiny hands and the groom's (slightly hairy) hands while saying 'Be happy and love long together.' I meant 'live long' but think 'love long' is a better slip of the tongue.

As I say this it occurs to me that I have been wandering around Thailand looking for a cat but my life is clearly offering me something else, and it is downright churlish to ignore it. I mean him. As the water continues to flow I realise that being with a man need not mean the disillusion of past relationships. In fact those past relationships are necessary so that you recognise someone nice when they come along, as Mo's sister clearly did from the happy look on her face. That independence is a state of mind, not an alliance with a cat. And in fact just because the one I found to love was in human rather than feline form was no reason to go and leave him.

I suddenly feel alive and awake and switched on and in the moment, and everything Claudius would like. I see their hands joined together clearly through the water. I pour it hastily, splashily, back and forth over them as I realise I *must* get home and find Cat Cam Man *immediately*. The water drips down to shining golden bowls adorned with floating lotus. Afterwards one of Mo's little sisters gives me a scented hankie as a memento of the wedding.

Aching to run to the nearest airport, I go to the enormous reception party, drinking and partying and dancing late into the night in celebration of my mental liberation. Not knowing anyone other than Mo means it's slightly lonesome, but realising that I cannot force the cat issue and that I'm going to give an adult relationship a chance, with Cat Cam Man if he's still around, puts me in a jittery, excited mood. Fantasies of dancing at parties with him, of doing trips around Southeast Asia with him, of downing cocktails with him fill my head, so that pretty soon I am laughing, chatting and nodding to myself as I put the final touches to my daydreams. This behaviour naturally draws the eye somewhat, but only smiles and friendly faces greet me, and finally Mo's younger brothers ask me to dance. Considering they are twelve and eight we make a very strange trio stomping around the dance floor.

Having booked my flight home, and tried to call Cat Cam Man (with only an answering machine and a nervous and uninformative 'Oh, er, hello!' left message) I give it one last chance at the cat show Martin Clutterbuck mentioned at the beginning of my trip, in the Rama Gardens Hotel. Except it turns out to be a dog show (serves me right) in front of a relative of the King, a niece or granddaughter, who sits under a tent surrounded by flowers and generals and ladies-in-waiting.

A string quartet in black-and-white-Dalmatian-pattern shirts plays *Fiddler on the Roof* and tango music while girls in fabulous pink frou-frou walk their dogs up a runway, the dogs dressed in matching fabulous pink frou-frou. Dressed as cowboys, or in platforms and flares, or as Bo Peep, or in sophisticated ball gowns, the girls adore their matching pooches. At prize-giving, a kneeling lady-in-waiting, her head bowed, presents boxes of chocs on a golden cup to the royal lady. She takes them without looking at the lady-in-waiting, and hands them to the recipient without a glance. She then grabs the next box and doles it out, looking utterly bored. Not once does her face crack into a smile.

I find a small area with cats and meander around inside the judging area. Every cattery owner I have met is gathered here. Sumali, Mr Aree, Ed from Chiang Mai, all with their best cats on show. And they're no match for the Khorats – or Claudius. There is one lovely Siamese kitten but – it's not for sale. The other cats are freaked by the noise (chickens are being judged in the next space along) and so not that keen on me sticking my fingers through their cages to stroke them. I'm like a girl who is too keen on a boy. You have to play a little hard to get with cats. I keep saying to myself as I lift them out of their cages without the owner's permission, well, if this one walks towards me maybe I'll take it . . . But it never does.

So, catless, I come home. But my journey isn't over. When I step off the plane I can't walk. Whatever my back has been working up to has happened. My right leg gives way under me, and I'm in agony. The pain is unspeakable. I spend one night moving every five seconds, unable to find a comfortable position where the pain would abate even for a moment. At three in the morning I'm on all fours on my kitchen floor howling like an animal, crying out for help. Next morning I have an MRI scan. Five days later I'm under the knife for a prolapsed disc.

As I come round from the anaesthetic, I'm given a morphine drip to combat the pain. Claudius is in the room, sitting in the armchair like a human, legs down and crossed, in a velvet jacket and smoking a pink Sobranie. He is distinctly at odds with the plain pine and chintzy inelegance of the hospital room.

'Darling, this will have to be quick as they're showing *Sunset Boulevard* in half an hour and I don't want to miss the beginning.'

'Claudius, were you gay?'

'Really, this seems to be a big issue for you – whether people are gay or not. You're like your mother.'

'Yes, ever since she died I feel more and more like her.'

'Well, of course it is inevitable. One always turns into one's parents in the end.'

He takes a long drag on the Sobranie and simultaneously lights up a yellow one.

'Oh dear,' I sigh morosely. 'My journey was a bit loserville. I didn't find my cat. And I'm now too ill to call my boyfriend. Or should I say my erstwhile boyfriend?'

'You remind me of a story my Buddhist teacher once told me. He said if you point out the moon to a cat, she probably won't look at the sky – she'll come up and sniff your finger. This is how you are. You're looking at the finger and not the sky.'

'I know. And you're looking at the world's worst Buddhist. Or Boodist as Dodie would say. I had a moment back at the wedding when I saw what you meant, but honestly. Perhaps I should stop trying to be something I'm not. A Buddhist! I mean, really!'

'Don't feel awful about the cat. You'll have another one day, but wait for the right time, let your cat find you.'

'So what's the point about the cat and the moon?'

'If you look at the whole, you see how everything works together, and how everything is fluid and not fixed as we would have it. And if everything is fluid it means change is a good and necessary thing. So let change happen.'

'Yes. And that means you're dead.'

He is silent.

'Well. I suppose I'm still alive.'

'Yes!'

'And that I'm fine as I am? Whole, I mean?'

'Yes!'

'And that only I can really save myself?'

'Of course. Now remember. Be awake! Keep awake! Be engaged with every moment. I wanted to say that before I said goodbye.'

'Oh,' I say disconsolately. 'Yes, you're right. It should be goodbye.'

'I must go because Greta Garbo's having your mother and me over for bridge at five.'

'But it's three in the morning.'

'Parallel universe. We're not on Greenwich Mean Time.'

'Don't go! I have more questions. How come you get to spend time with the glitterati? And is it really an advanced cocktail party up there?'

'For some of us,' he says ominously, implying, I can't

help feeling, that I'll never be invited to enough parties, ever.

'*Oh!* They're dealing the cards. Now *wake up!*'

And he's gone. And I do.

Next morning my surgeon visits.

'Any problems, Miss de Vries?'

'Actually, Mr Adam, yes. My cat, who is dead, seems to
think he's Noël Coward. My mother, who is also dead, is
more interested in playing bridge with Greta Garbo than
coming to see me. My back, which is kaput, has rendered
me unable to face my man. And I have developed an ability
to digest jewels.'

He looks puzzled, but frowns, and after a moment's
thought says, 'Remember that essentially the next world
is one of dreams. Sometimes things work smoothly, fast
you fly from one scene to the next, but at others you
are swimming through treacle. We are all trying to get to
each other – and even though we might be right there,
because of the time travel we cannot see each other. And
the same goes with our search for love on this plane. Your
mother is in fact with you, just the other side of the ether,
and she may at this moment be longing to swim through
to you, but the time translation makes it seem as though
she is miles away playing bridge with dead film stars.'

'And why do we always dream of dead film stars as our
friends?'

'Because we hate to admit we are normal.'

He walks out. Seconds later he walks back in.

'Ah good morning. How are you feeling, Miss de Vries?'

★   ★   ★

Now as I lie recovering, I have almost turned into a cat myself. I sleep six hours a day, at least, and I'm at my best between five and seven in the morning. But I don't have the flexible back of a cat. Actually I can barely walk. And this makes me angry because being supine and ill is hardly the sexiest way to entice a man you've already left once into going back out with you. The pain is boring and debilitating. But eventually I think: This is ridiculous, I don't want to wait any more. As the phantom surgeon said, we are all trying to get to one another. So I call Cat Cam Man. He comes to see me in hospital. As we chat he makes me laugh. He takes my anger away. To me it is an armour of iron but to him it's just a fur-trimmed evening stole.

He then drives me home from the hospital, which is sweet, especially considering I have to put the seat back as far as it will go, so whenever he opens his mouth it looks as though he's some nutter talking to himself. He broaches the subject of cats.

'So how likely are you to be rushing off to Ethiopia to look for an Abyssinian in the near future?'

'Not very likely.'

'I mean, if your back allowed you to.'

'Nope. I love cats. Yes. But in Thailand the more I searched, the less I found. It made me recognise that my desperate need for a cat was just that – desperate. I was looking for a special bond, an instant click, a feeling that isn't manufacturable. Then when I *did* feel that in Sukhothai, I wasn't allowed to have the kittens I'd found. I realised that the time was right for me to focus my energies elsewhere.

I try throwing him a meaningful come-hither look, but my eyes slide around as though I'm on drugs, so I stop it.

'I think I was well on my way to being one of those people – and not all cat-lovers are like this – who want a cat as an emotional stop gap. I just want to be someone who loves cats, without thinking that unless I have one I'm not whole. Because that's ridiculous. Hello? Are you still awake?'

'Yes. Just thinking.'

After a silence he suggests we go out together again, and even though this is what I want, I still experience a tremor of fear, like a cat's paw rippling a pond. Of course just because I think this is love doesn't mean it is. After all the journeying, I wonder if I can face the hope and the fear. Do I have the energy to have my heart broken again if that's what comes? Cats predict earthquakes hours before they happen, running crazily around houses, trying to get out. I feel slightly similar but only because when I review the kings in my life they've never been the king of hearts, only the king of spades. But things can change. I'm bored with not trusting, of not having faith. Do I have the energy? Sure I do. Of course I do. Come on *nats*, throw at me what you can: no cats, broken backs, love spats. I can handle it.

So I say yes.

But there are very few spats. In fact there are so few that I wonder if I've become a different person. I still think about the kittens in Sukhothai and feel the way I did when I left Cat Cam Man for Thailand – yearning – but there's nothing I can do about it so I carry on being happy.

On New Year's Eve, we spend a quiet evening in the country by the fire. Cat Cam Man walks out and a few minutes later comes back in.

'Why don't you come outside?' he says.

Outside the air is icy. Frost covers the garden. Cat Cam Man looks expectant and embarrassed but my attention is taken by the moon.

'Look! I've never seen this before!' I squeal.

'Yes! Oh! What?'

'The moon! Look at it. It has a rainbow around it.'

'Mmm. Beautiful.'

'What's happened?'

'The light of the moon is refracting through the frozen ice crystals of a very high cloud. But isn't that more beautiful?'

He points down to a cardboard box.

'No, that's rubbish,' I say absent-mindedly. Looking again I see holes in the box. I pick it up and open it. Inside is a kitten wrapped in blankets and towels. We take the box inside.

'I couldn't decide which breed to get. So I got a mixture of both. She's half Siamese and half Burmese.'

'Tonkinese?'

'Yes, that's right.'

'She's beautiful.'

'Happy New Year, darling.'

'Can I get out now?'

'Of course you can.'

'I can what?'

'Get out.'

'Get out? You want me to get out? From my own home? After giving you a kitten?'

'Not you, darling.'

'Oh.'

'Do you know your name?'

'Er yes, don't you?'

'Honky!' she squeaks.

'Honky?'

'Sorry?'

'Yes!'

She twirls round, very over-excited. 'Honky! Honky! Honky!'

'OK. As you're a girl I don't think we can call you Claudius.'

I turn to Cat Cam Man.

'Thank you so much, darling.'

'You're welcome. Now then. I've got this tiny camera I was thinking of fixing to her collar . . .'

But I'm not concentrating. Honky Tonk and I are kissing each other hello.

BIBLIOGRAPHY

The Legend of Siamese Cats, Martin R. Clutterbuck (White Lotus Press, 1998).

Cat World, A Feline Encyclopaedia, Desmond Morris (Ebury Press, 1996).

Thailand, Eyewitness Travel Guide (Dorling Kindersley, 1997).

Myanmar (Burma), Michael Clark and Joe Cummings (Lonely Planet Publications, 2000).

Burmese Folk Tales, Maung Htin Aung (Oxford University Press, 1959).

Golden Earth, Travels in Burma, Norman Lewis (Eland, 1983).

The Traveller's History of Burma, Gerry Abbott (Orchid Press, 1998).

Burma Then and Now, Nicholas Greenwood (Bradt Publications, 1993).

Freedom from Fear, Aung San Suu Kyi (Penguin Books, 1995).

Letters from Burma, Aung San Suu Kyi (Penguin Books, 1997).

Under the Dragon, Travels in a Betrayed Land, Rory Maclean (Flamingo, 1999).

Buddhism, Plain and Simple, Steve Hagen (Penguin Books, 1999).

The Revolutionary King, The True-Life Sequel to the King and I, William Stevenson (Constable, 1999).

Thai Ways, Denis Segaller (Post Books, 1998).

More Thai Ways, Denis Segaller (Post Books, 2000).

A World Overturned, Maureen Baird-Murray (Constable & Company, 1997).

Burmese Days, George Orwell (Penguin, 1989).

Twilight over Burma: My Life as a Shan Princess, Inge Sargent (University of Hawaii Press, 1994).

A Fortune Teller Told Me, Tiziano Terzani (Flamingo, 1998).

More Burma Women's Voices (The Thanakha Team, 1998).

Outrage: Burma's Struggle for Democracy, Bertil Lintner (White Lotus Press, 1990).

Borderlines: A Journey Through Burma and Thailand, Charles Nicholl (Secker & Warburg, 1988).

Forgotten Land: A Rediscovery of Burma, Harriet O'Brien (Michael Joseph, 1991).

Jasmine Nights, S. P. Somtow (Hamish Hamilton, 1994).

A NOTE ON THE AUTHOR

Clare de Vries is a freelance journalist
and travel writer. Her first book *I &
Claudius* is published by Bloomsbury.

A NOTE ON THE TYPE

The text of this book is set in Bembo.
The type was first used in 1495 by the
Venetian printer Aldus Manutius for
Cardinal Bembo's *De Aetna*, and was
cut for Manutius by Francesco Griffo.
It was one of the types used by Claude
Garamond (1480–1561) as a model for
his Romain de L'Université, and so
it was the forerunner of what became
standard European type for the
following two centuries. Its modern
form follows the original types and
was designed for Monotype in 1929.